Out of My Mind

Books by Richard Armour

It All Started with Marx
It All Started with Stones and Clubs
My Life with Women
Out of My Mind
A Safari into Satire
A Short History of Sex
Through Darkest Adolescence
Twisted Tales from Shakespeare
Writing Light Verse and Prose Humor

FOR CHILDREN
The Adventures of Egbert the Easter Egg
All Sizes and Shapes of Monkeys and Apes
Animals on the Ceiling
A Dozen Dinosaurs
Odd Old Mammals
On Your Marks: A Package of Punctuation
Our Presidents
Who's in Holes?
The Year Santa Went Modern

OUT OF
MY
MIND

By Richard Armour

McGRAW-HILL BOOK COMPANY

New York   Toronto   St. Louis

Düsseldorf   Mexico   Panama

FIRST EDITION

DESIGNED AT THE INKWELL STUDIO

Armour, Richard Willard,
    Out of my Mind.

    I. Title.
PS3501.R55084   818'.5'207   77-38547
ISBN 0-07-002297-6

Acknowledgments

The material in this book, except for the Afterthoughts, originally appeared in the following publications: "The Other Side of the Coin" in *American Youth;* "Booked for Bed" in *Carte Blanche;* "My Hong Kong Tailor Is Better than Your Hong Kong Tailor" in *Escapade;* "Confessions of a Cold-Cure Collector" and "Who Says I'm Hard of Hearing?" in *Family Health;* "Yes, Virginia, There Is a Thanksgiving" in *Family Weekly;* "Discovery of an Unpublished Manuscript" and "Reading for a Desert Island" in *The Journal of the American Medical Association;* "And So to Beds" and "A Short History of the Embrace" in *Knight;* "Incident in Japan" in *Nugget;* "The Conversation Game and How to Win It," "Oh, to Be Twenty-Twenty Again," "Something to Worry About," "Their Breath Is Sweet, Their Skin Is Pure," "Time and Time Again," "Treasure on the Beach," and "Have You Ever Given Much Thought to a Paper Clip?" in *Orange County Illustrated;* "Color Me Blue" in

vii

Orange County Sun; "Every Day Is Father's Day" and "Houses I Have Known and Loved" in *Parents' Magazine;* "The Depopulation Explosion," "Looking Over the Overlooked Elbow," "Science Marches On," and "A Short Dissertation on Lips" in *Playboy;* "The Author on TV" and "And Make It a Sonnet, If You Don't Mind" in *Publishers' Weekly;* "They Won't *Let* Me Stop Smoking" in *Reader's Digest;* "Add a Word," "Backward, Turn Backward," "Consider the Artichoke," "Going to the Dog," "Fountain of My Youth," "Long Distance Doesn't Lend Enchantment," " 'N'," "Reading Habits of the Young," "A Short Note on Hair," "Watch Out," and "Why I Never Celebrate Library Week" in Martin Levin's "The Phoenix Nest," *Saturday Review.* Grateful acknowledgment is made to all concerned for permission to include these writings in this book.

Contents

Foreword

John Milton, who must have been ambidextrous, said he wrote poetry with his right hand and prose with his left. I wish I had lived in the seventeenth century, so that I might have stood behind him, watching him write *Paradise Lost* and *The Doctrine and Discipline of Divorce* simultaneously.

As for me, I am unable to write even a couplet and a simple sentence at the same time. Using two typewriters makes it no easier. But then, I am not a genius like Milton and Shakespeare. My life contains no Horton Period or Lost Years, my works are not on the Required Reading List, and there is no course called Introduction to Armour, a prerequisite for Armour 121a,b.

Yet I do write both verse and prose. The verse has been collected in several volumes and read by several people. But the prose, though calm, is not collected. I have friends who are coin collectors, stamp collectors, shell collectors —even garbage collectors. But I know no prose collectors, so I have had to collect all this prose myself.

Prose is defined as "the ordinary language of men in speaking or writing; opposed to verse." What I have brought together in this volume must be prose, because it is about as ordinary language as you will find, but I do not think it is opposed to verse. I know I am not. I am, however, opposed to many things, as will be seen by anyone who reads this book. I am in favor of some things, too, as will be seen by anyone who reads this book closely.

Most of these pieces are very short. I exhaust my knowledge of a subject rather quickly. Years ago I read an advertisement for a self-improvement course that I probably should have taken. The advertisement asked, "Have you a grasshopper mind?" The course was guaranteed to take a mind that hopped all over, from one subject to another, and get it to settle down. At the time, I was not ready to settle down, and now it is too late. But I am not hopping mad, I am hopping happy. One advantage of exhausting my knowledge of a subject quickly is that I write short pieces that do not exhaust the reader, unless the reader exhausts easily.

That is about all that needs to be said here except to point out that each piece in this book has, instead of an introduction, an extraduction. I considered such descriptive terms for it as postscript, appendage, tailpiece, coda, addendum, and supplement, but finally decided to call the thing an afterthought. After reading a few of these afterthoughts, you may think of something else to call them. If you do, please do not tell me.

These are only a few of the prose pieces I have written over the years. Obviously, I have not included the best of them.

R. A.

Treasure on the Beach

One hot summer day I was lying on the beach, wondering why some people get a tan and others get freckles. Suddenly I heard a loud clicking noise a few feet in back of me. I got up onto one elbow, turned my head around, and saw a tall, middle-aged woman stoop over and scoop up some sand in a wire mesh cup. The sand trickled through the mesh, leaving an object in the bottom that she fished out and put into a small bag that hung from her shoulder. The clicking sound stopped.

Then I saw that the clicking had come from a long-handled instrument with a flat metal disk at one end. It looked like a mine detector. As I watched, the woman started moving slowly away, keeping the disk close to the sand.

My curiosity, which arouses easily, was aroused. I got up and walked over to the woman. I could see now that she had some sort of magnetic device and was probing the sand.

"Lost something?" I asked.

"No, just looking," she said. "This thing locates any metal object."

"What have you found today?"

"A nickel, three pennies, and six bobby pins. But I've been out here only two hours."

That's eight cents for two hours or four cents an hour, I thought to myself. Not a very good way to make a living, unless she can sell the bobby pins to a beauty parlor or melt them down and make them into something useful, assuming the bobby pins are no longer any good for pinning bobbies.

The detecting device was clicking again. The woman scooped up the sand directly under where the disk had been and shook the cup back and forth, like a miner panning for gold. When all the sand had run out, a small object was left.

"What is it?" I asked. "Anything valuable?"

"A metal button," she said, dropping it into her bag. Maybe she didn't throw it back on the sand because she might pick it up again. Or maybe, as I began to suspect, some of her buttons were missing.

"What's the most valuable thing you've ever found?" I asked.

"A fifty-cent piece," she said, with a trace of pride in her voice.

"Well, maybe you haven't been at it long."

"A little over a year."

"How much does one of those magnetic devices cost?" Not that I was thinking of buying one, but I just like to know such things.

"About $150," she said. "I don't know exactly. My husband gave it to me for a birthday present."

"Oh, I see," I said. And I *was* beginning to see. Her husband probably gave it to her to keep her busy. Perhaps she was always phoning him at the office. Perhaps she spent all her spare time shopping and running up bills. An expenditure of $150, plus the small cost for recharging the battery every few months, would be cheap enough and might save many times that much.

We were walking along the beach. Every now and then the machine would start clicking and the woman would scoop out the sand with her wire mesh cup and shake the cup from side to side and take out the object left in the bottom. There was always something. The machine never made a mistake. Once, when the clicking had been unusually loud, it was a ballpoint pen, so corroded as to be useless. Another time it was an empty .22 cartridge. And once it was a safety pin.

"Not much cash today," I said.

"No," she said, "but it's early yet."

The machine started clicking. Once again the woman went through the process of scooping and sifting.

"Look!" she exclaimed triumphantly, holding up a coin. "A dime."

"Congratulations," I said.

This rich discovery spurred the woman on. I could hardly keep up with her as she darted about. Nor was she very considerate of others. Once she got so close to a sleeping sunbather that she awakened him with the clicking.

"Would you mind moving your head a little?" she asked him.

Almost before he moved, she started scooping out the sand next to his face. She thought she had found something big. She had. It was a coffee can, almost as good as new but unfortunately without any coffee in it.

I was beginning to get into the spirit of the thing. There was something compelling about it. No telling what might be lying there under the sand. A diamond ring. Spanish doubloons, washed up from a pirate ship that went down off the coast. Something of sentimental value for which a huge reward was offered.

I had come to notice gradations of tone and of speed of clicking. Though uninvited, I felt like a partner in the enterprise. I applauded each find. I began to suggest places to search.

"I'm going to lunch," the woman said after a while. "You can use it until I get back. Just turn it on and off with this little switch. Don't go too far away. I'll be back in half an hour."

So I was left with the metal detector. I started slowly working my way down the beach, full of great expectations. Each time the machine started clicking, my heart started pounding. Once I found a nail, in excellent condition. As soon as the rust is removed, it will be quite usable. Once I found a hinge, probably from the lid of a lunch basket. A little oil, and it will be ready to swing again. I found two hair curlers, a nail file, and—my most exciting discovery—a perfectly good belt buckle.

The owner of the detecting contraption came back from lunch. I was so preoccupied with my work that I had forgotten all about eating.

"Any luck?" she asked.

"Just fair," I said, trying to be modest.

"Let's see," she said.

So I showed her the nail and the hinge and the hair curlers and all the rest. I was pretty proud of myself. All of this in only half an hour.

"Hand them over," she said.

"But I found them," I said.

"It's my machine," she said.

I begged her to let me keep the belt buckle, but she shook her head.

"Anything found with my machine is mine," she said, and there was a look in her eyes that frightened me. I handed everything over and didn't argue any more. Hunting for treasure brings out something mean and possessive in people.

I lay down on the beach again, and I heard the ticking grow fainter and fainter. Weary from all that walking and scooping, and a little faint myself from having had no lunch, I dozed off. I dreamed about being a Forty-Niner prospecting for gold, and I had a barroom brawl with an old harridan known as Mother Lode and shot her dead.

AFTERTHOUGHT:

The most important thing at a beach, other than girls (to men) and men (to girls), is sand. If you think you may ever be called upon to explain the difference between sand, gravel, and silt, you had better pay close attention to the next few sentences. Gravel is the same thing as sand but larger. It is particles of rock that are more than two millimeters in diameter, while sand is particles of rock that are less than two millimeters in diameter. But sand mustn't get too small. If it gets under one-sixteenth of a millimeter in diameter, it is considered silt. And being considered silt must be a frightful comedown for any self-respecting grain of sand.

Sand has a tendency to get into things, and this, I think, is going to have far-reaching consequences. Little by little, sand is being carried away from beaches in people's hair and ears and trouser cuffs. In time, if this keeps up, all of the sand will have been carried inland and there will be none at beaches.

Some hope is provided by cuffless trousers. But offsetting this is longer hair, and beards. Happily, however, there is one stable element. Ears retain their traditional capacity, carrying off about the same amount of sand year after year or, we might say, ear after ear.

Shake your hair, clean out your ears. The next time you leave the beach, try your best to leave it.

Add a Word

It has always seemed to me that the epitome of fame is to become a noun in the dictionary. Think of the immortality of James Watt, who gave us the watt, Alessandro Volta, from whom we have the volt, and A. M. Ampère, father of the ampere, more familiarly known as the amp. Also in the field of science, where this sort of thing seems to be most common, consider the Bunsen burner, which causes the name of Professor R. W. Bunsen of Heidelberg to live on. And Fahrenheit, which we owe to Gabriel Daniel Fahrenheit, the German physicist who improved the thermometer by substituting mercury for alcohol in the tube.

Medical men like James Parkinson, the English physician who gave us Parkinson's disease (that is, he gave us the name of it), and Thomas Addison, without whom we would not know what to call Addison's disease, are also well, if not happily, remembered. Less familiar to the layman but known by any physician is Dr. Charles Mc-

Burney, the American surgeon who gave his name to McBurney's point. This is the place on the ventral abdominal wall where the most acute pain is elicited by pressure in cases of appendicitis. Vidkun Quisling, the pro-Nazi Norwegian fifth columnist, got into the dictionary with the noun quisling, such a satisfying and useful word that in time we may expect the verb to quisle. Of course Napoleon's devoted follower Nicolas Chauvin, long ago gave us chauvinism; and Lord Raglan, the British general, the raglan sleeve. From John L. McAdam, a Scottish engineer, we have a word to describe the pavement on our highways, and from the inventive Benjamin Franklin we have, among other things, the open stove that bears his name.

All this is leading up to my nomination of a word to be incorporated into the English language. The man it would memorialize is not a scientist, a physician, a traitor, an overenthusiastic patriot, a general, an engineer, or a statesman. But his name has long seemed to me to supply a need in our vocabulary. I refer to James Thurber. It is true that the American botanist G. Thurber (1821–1890) has already given us *Thurberia thespesioides*. But James Thurber, one of my favorite authors, deserves to be in the dictionary all on his own, and lower case.

What I propose is the noun thurb. I also suggest the adjective thurb, of which thurber (as in the author's name) is the comparative and thurbest the superlative. And the verb to thurb: I thurb, you thurb, he (she, it) thurbs, we thurb, you (plural) thurb, they thurb. The word thurber could also be a noun, meaning one who thurbs.

As for the meaning of thurb, I look on it as an all-purpose word. It can mean anything one wishes it to, supplying the need of the moment. Note how effectively it serves in the following sentences:

He cleaned out his trouser cuffs, removing all the accumulated thurb.

A lot of thurbing is going on in some of our government agencies.

He told the doctor he had a good night's sleep and is feeling a little thurber this morning.

"Oh, thurb!" he exclaimed. "I left my wallet in my other coat."

She watched him thurb his way through the traffic until he was lost from sight.

It was a clear day, except for a little thurbishness over the mountains.

If James Watt can get into the dictionary for giving us a unit of power, surely James Thurber should get in there for all he has given us. In the dictionary, I might add, thurb would come just after thuoc, an Annamese unit of measure. If the dictionary is already too crowded to admit thurb, just drop out thuoc, a word that not many would miss. It's something to thurb about, anyhow.

AFTERTHOUGHT:

Readers who have written me about this usually close their letters with "Thurberly yours," or, when they are being formal, "I remain, yours thurberly." One who liked my little article said, "It was delightful. Thurb you very much." But a rather testy gentleman, thinking I was taking Thurber's name in vain, exploded, "I could kick you right smack in the thurb!" I cherish a letter in which the reader proposed establishment of a new religious sect, to be called Thurberian. "We Thurberians," he wrote, "would be Protestant, in fact inclined to protest vigorously about such things as war and women, as did our founder, James Thurber. A Thurberian minister would not so much preach as give a chalk talk, illustrating his remarks with absurd drawings imitating those appearing in early texts of our Bible, *The New Yorker*."

Having reread my article, I see that I made one mistake. I said that the comparative of the adjective thurb is thurber, as in the author's name. But I realize now that this could not be. Thurber was unquestionably superlative. However, unless his name was originally Thurbest, changed by some modest forebear to Thurber, I must give some other explanation. I fall back, therefore, on the fact that Thurber, like other names ending in *-er* or *-or,* is a *nomen agentis,* or name of one who does something. Thus, Fisher is one who fishes, Baker is one who bakes, and Thurber is one who thurbs. There is no need to be comparative about it. When it came to thurbing, James Thurber was the greatest. I am absolutely thurb about it.

One more thing. I received a delightful letter from Helen Thurber, James Thurber's widow. "Your idea is a lovely one," she wrote. "But it seems more likely to me that the word 'mitty' will some day get into the dictionary."

Actually mitty is already in the dictionary. It's a local word in England, referring to a dark-colored, white-rumped bird which, because it is supposed to be a harbinger of bad weather, is known as a stormy petrel. I probably should have told Mrs. Thurber about this but I didn't have the thurb to do so.

Why I Never
Celebrate Library Week

The only time I have ever had any trouble with librarians was when I was about eight years old. I had had a library card since I was six, and for two years had been taking out the maximum number of books and unfailingly returning them before the date they were due. I was a good citizen, a timid little boy who made no difficulty for his parents, his teachers, or those who dispense books at the public library.

Then one day I received a blunt, coldly indignant note from the librarian. A book signed out by me had been returned in mutilated condition, and the cost of purchasing a new copy as a replacement must be paid at once or my card would be revoked.

The word "mutilated" was new to me, my vocabulary at that time not containing some of the words which, unfortunately, have been added since. But my father quickly made it clear. When I understood, I was shocked. I had never mutilated anything, except once when I had pulled two legs off an ant to see if it could still walk (it could), and afterward was very sorry and tried to put them back on (I couldn't). Besides, I liked books better than ants. After all, they didn't sting, or crawl all over your sandwich at a picnic.

"I didn't do it," I said to my father. "Cross my heart and hope to die. I didn't do it."

"But it says here you did," said my father, inclined to believe written evidence, any time, as against the oral testimony of his only son.

However, it was not my mutilating a book that raised my father's eyebrows, and would have raised the librarian's if they had not already been as high as they would go. What disturbed my father, and especially the librarian, was what this particular book, signed out by an eight-year-old boy of supposedly good character, was about.

It was a book about bees. Indeed, it was a large (and expensive) book about bees, and it told absolutely everything about them, including their sex life, which I have since come to understand is a little irregular. I had been told about the birds, and now, on my own, I apparently had learned about the bees. Knowing about both the birds and the bees, I would seem to know everything, or at least too much for an eight-year-old.

I swear to this day that I not only didn't mutilate that book, I didn't even sign it out. Someone, I insist, stole my library card and forged my signature. It was probably a sex maniac, lusting to read a nasty book and driven to desperate measures.

Anyhow, my father paid for the replacement of the book, taking it out of my allowance. When I say he took it out of my allowance, I mean I got no more allowance for thirteen weeks, the book being that costly and my allowance that small.

But worst of all was the way that librarian turned

against me. She began keeping tabs on the books I signed out, standing over me and looking grim and suspicious. To her, I was a bad boy, forever hunting out books that would add to my already large stock of knowledge about the facts of life.

Though I never again got into serious trouble with librarians, I am still a little uneasy when around them. I have a feeling they know all about my past.

AFTERTHOUGHT:

Despite the injustice done me in the matter of the book about the bees, I am not one to hold a grudge. I have never burned my library card, nor have I incited others to burn theirs. Some of my best friends are librarians. True, I have written some uncomplimentary verses about librarians. But then, I have written in the same vein, part jocular and part jugular, about doctors, dentists, lawyers, bankers, professors, postmen, waiters, and just about everyone, including my wife, my children, and myself. Here are some lines about one curious habit of librarians:

> Librarians with tender tread
> Slip past the reader, bowed of head,
> And only rouse him from his book
> And cause a dark, distracted look
> When, righteously incensed and stirred,
> They "Shush!" some person he's not heard.

Fountain of My Youth

It has just occurred to me that there are young people growing up today who have never had the experience of using a fountain pen. All they know is a ballpoint. I haven't used a fountain pen for many years myself, but I remember what it was like.

A fountain pen, for those who have never seen one, had liquid ink inside, sloshing around. I know this sounds improbable, but it is true. Such a pen was filled by holding the point in a bottle of ink or an inkwell, working a lever so that it would press down on a rubber sack, and then releasing the lever, permitting the rubber sack to expand and suck in the ink. If, before filling it, the pen was thought to be empty but wasn't, and the lever was worked, a stream of ink would squirt out, inundating anyone or anything in its path. That is why it is called a fountain pen.

Of course, carrying around a pen full of ink could be hazardous business. I remember once when my fountain pen for some reason disgorged its contents while I was carrying it in my shirt pocket. The stain never came out, ink removers being less effective in those days, and I went around holding my hand over the spot. People thought I was taking an oath or perhaps swearing allegiance to the flag.

Unlike the ballpoint pen, which requires a cartridge refill, a fountain pen could be filled anywhere there was a supply of ink. I filled my own pen at the post office, though the ink was not of the best quality and had a kind of linty encrustation. Another source of ink was a bank. At banks, however, the inkwells were cannily made so shallow that, though they served very well for dipping, they prevented a capacity filling. Sometimes I would draw up a bubble and have to expel it, the way a doctor does with a hypodermic before thrusting it into a patient.

One advantage of a fountain pen was in writing one's signature. It was possible to get a flourish that the ballpoint could never produce. Even after the ballpoint came into use, I kept a fountain pen on my desk for several years, just for my signature. Now, however, I have gone over to the ballpoint entirely, and my signature is not only without character but almost legible.

One thing you can't get with a ballpoint is a blot— the result of a sudden, unexpected outpouring that left a pool of ink and confronted you with the problem of what to do with it. My own method was to use the corner of a blotter and depend on capillary attraction. It was a delicate operation, because if anything went amiss, the ink would run down the page. I became an expert in the use of a blotter, and took a certain pride in blotting an ink spot without enlarging it. (By the way, I haven't seen a blotter for years.)

The fountain pen I remember best was a large green one that had my name on it in gold letters. It held an enormous amount of ink, and could go for weeks without refilling. It was also capable of producing really king-size blots, some of which would fill all four corners of a blotter, and put my skill to the ultimate test.

The large green fountain pen came to a sad end. Somehow it fell to the floor, unnoticed, and I stepped on it. I distinctly recall the crunching sound it made, as if I had stepped on some brittle creature, such as a snail or a grasshopper. The ink spurted in every direction, like strangely dark blood, and I felt that I had unwittingly taken an innocent life.

Perhaps it is just as well I no longer have a fountain pen. Both the post office and the bank now use ballpoint pens, and if I had a fountain pen I don't know where I could fill it.

AFTERTHOUGHT:

Fountain pens used to carry the name of the maker, such as Parker or Schaeffer, but ballpoint pens bear the name of the donor, such as United Savings and Loan, Henderson Insurance, Tri-City Feed and Fuel, and Gibson Mortuary. Once I used my ballpoint pen to sign a wedding book and must have put it down and picked up a pen belonging to someone else. That is how I lost my perfectly good Acme Florists and became the owner of a Kilzum Pest Control, with its slogan "Doc Kilzum, His Patients All Die." I tried to get rid of this one, but every time I left it behind, someone would come running up to me and say, "Didn't you forget your pen?"

Sometimes I think I would rather buy a ballpoint pen than advertise the Setting Sun Rest Home or Extra Fine Fertilizers. But I shall do nothing rash.

Science Marches On

These days, unless you can talk about science you are out of it—sidetracked in conversations and frowned upon when you try to get the subject around to something you are up on, such as sex. Hence this historical survey, which I hope will prove helpful.

The word science comes from the Latin *scire,* meaning to know; and now that you know this, you can impress people who don't know what the word science comes from. In German, the word for science is *Wissenschaft,* which, interestingly enough, is feminine. You might keep this in mind the next time you see an attractive young laboratory assistant leaning over her microscope in a low-cut blouse.

One of the most important discoveries in early times was the discovery of fire. It is not known who discovered fire, unless you believe all that jazz about Prometheus, but I would assume that his first word on making the discovery was not "Eureka!" but "Ouch!" The discovery of fire led to many improvements, such as fire alarms, fire sales, and fire insurance. It also brought about central heating, which at first was accomplished by setting fire to the center of the house and letting it spread outward. Before houses were heated, people went to bed to get warm, which was more fun than sitting around talking.

Shortly after the discovery of fire came the discovery of the wheel, which was essential to the fire engine. The first wheel was probably a round stone with a hole in the center. When a prehistoric inventor took two of these stones and put one in front of the other and asked a friend what this reminded him of, the friend thought a moment and then said, "A bicycle." After this, it was no trick at all to put four such stones together and build the first wagon. It was, however, not a station wagon but a stationary wagon, since it was too heavy to move. In time, with wheels of lighter construction, vehicles of various kinds took to the road and there were the crude beginnings of a traffic problem. With invention of the back seat, there was a dramatic rise in population.

One of the most famous of early scientists was Archimedes. A Greek mathematician, he discovered the laws of the lever and boasted, "Give me a place to stand on and I will move the earth!" Unable to find such a place, he had to content himself with experiments that led to the invention of the Archimedean screw.

One day when Archimedes was in the public bath, he noticed that the more his body was immersed, the more water ran over the sides. He got others to do the same thing, both men and women, to be sure this was no fluke; and every time a young woman gradually lowered herself into the bath and the water spilled over, he got more excited. People were growing tired of getting in and out, and the floor was a mess, but Archimedes had discovered that a body in water displaces an amount of water equal to its own bulk. Shortly thereafter he wrote a work entitled *On Floating Bodies,* which would have sold better had there been illustrations.

Another great scientist of the ancient world was Ptolemy, who insisted that the earth was at the center of the universe and was immovable. If the earth moved, he argued quite logically, things would fall off. Even the air, which was lighter, would be left behind. His Ptolemaic system was accepted for centuries, and there are those of us who still prefer it to the newfangled ideas about the universe.

Ptolemy also distinguished himself as a geographer. His eight-volume work contained maps of all the known parts of the world and was the standard textbook of geography until Columbus and other navigators, who went out and had a look, proved that Ptolemy had almost everything wrong. It was Ptolemy's good fortune, as both an astronomer and a geographer, to die before his errors were discovered.

During the Middle Ages, science was at a low point. Knights were so busy galloping around, looking for damsels to distress, that they had no time for controlled experiments. Serfs were so busy prostrating themselves before their masters that most of them had prostrate trouble. The only libraries that had not been burned were those in monasteries, where you had to agree to spend your life before you were issued a library card.

In 1101 A.D., with the establishment of the University of Paris, Paris became a seat of learning, though there were those who sat or lay around doing other things. Out of consideration for those who came from other countries, lectures were given in Latin instead of French. Students who had barely slid through elementary Latin were puzzled by some of the nuances of lectures in metaphysics.

The greatest scientist of the Middle Ages was Roger

Bacon. Bacon was so far ahead of his time in his scientific ideas that he was thought a magician. He insisted that he wasn't ahead, others were behind, and explained this by pointing out errors in the calendar. However, he was imprisoned without books or instruments, a frustrating experience for a scientist. Since this was in Paris, it would have been frustrating enough even for the ordinary tourist.

Chemistry took an interesting turn in the Middle Ages, when it was in the hands of alchemists. The alchemists were mostly concerned with only two things: (1) turning base metals into gold and (2) discovering a way of living forever. The two went together, because it was going to take plenty of money to live so many years after sixty-five with no Social Security or Medicare.

Great strides were made by science during the Renaissance. First there was Copernicus, who discovered that the earth rotates around the sun. Having no telescope, he figured this out by looking through slits in the walls of his home. What his neighbors saw by looking through these same slits, we can only conjecture.

Then there was Galileo, also known as Galileo Galilei by those who were a little uncertain and trying to get it right the second time if not the first. Galileo was interested in falling bodies, and hung around under towers and tall buildings, hoping. While he was not the inventor of the telescope, he was the first to make practical use of it, looking through it at the moon, the stars, and people who had no idea he could see what they were doing. He claimed not to be a Peeping Tom, because he was only making scientific experiments, but women were well advised to pull down their shades before starting to undress, unless they were exhibitionists. Galileo himself was well clothed, refusing to look at things with a naked eye.

Galileo's most famous experiment was dropping a ten-pound and a one-pound weight from the Tower of Pisa. This proved that a leaning tower is good for something after all. Galileo was placed under house arrest, not because one of his weights had hit a pedestrian on the head but because some of his ideas were so revolutionary. For instance, he maintained that anything that is not stationary is in motion. And he claimed to see spots on the sun, when obviously he hadn't cleaned his glasses.

In the seventeenth century there was Isaac Newton, who made some important discoveries after being hit on the head by an apple. Galileo had used a telescope to look through, but Newton built a reflecting telescope to do his serious thinking for him. One of Newton's theories was that all particles of matter in the universe exert an attraction on one another. What he did not realize is that this is especially true in the case of male and female particles. Though Newton, a bachelor, never knew it, he was very close to the discovery of sex.

A significant application of science came in the eighteenth century, when James Watt developed the steam engine. Watt is said to have got the idea from watching the steam come out of his mother's teakettle. The whistle it made reminded him of the whistle on a train; and once he had this in mind, he wouldn't rest until he had perfected the steam engine. The unit of power, the watt, is named after Watt, though some think it should have been named after Joseph Black, his predecessor. The next time you replace a burned-out 60-watt bulb, you might think of this.

It was about this time that scientists made advances in electricity. By flying a kite, Benjamin Franklin proved that lightning is electricity and not something else, such as an angry god. People laughed when they saw Franklin, a grown man, flying a kite in the midst of a rainstorm, but it has always been the fate of scientists and inventors to be laughed at. Fortunately, Franklin had not read the statement of a later scientist to the effect that "all bodies are capable of electrification," a discovery that was to be a boon to capital punishment.

In the early nineteenth century, Sir Humphry Davy for the first time isolated the chemical elements sodium and potassium, which for some reason was desirable. More obviously important was his coining the name chlorine for what had previously been called "dephlogisticated spirit of salt." This was almost as appropriate as calling the miner's safety lamp he invented the Davy lamp.

Davy was, and continues to be, a controversial figure. There are two schools of thought, one insisting on spelling his first name Humphrey and the other just as insistent that it be spelled Humphry. Davy, who married a wealthy woman and spent his last years traveling in Italy, the Tyrol, and Switzerland, refused to be drawn into the controversy.

Davy's assistant and successor was Michael Faraday. By running electric currents through all sorts of things, he developed the galvanometer, a device to measure the quantity of electricity. When he came out with his ballistic galvanometer, many thought he had gone a little too far. Indeed some, when they saw Faraday approaching, took to their heels. As if this were not enough, Faraday claimed to have discovered self-induction, though many insisted that this had been going on for centuries.

Davy often said that his greatest discovery was Faraday, and Faraday seems not to have taken offense.

Passing with some difficulty over such names as Kirchhoff, Hittorf, Boltzmann, and Hasenöhrl, we come to Einstein, whose theory of relativity I wouldn't understand even if I explained it to you. More recently there have been scientists such as Fleming, the discoverer of

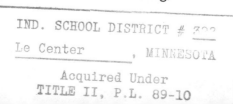

penicillin, and Salk, the discoverer of the fact that some people would rather have polio than stand in line to get a shot.

Modern science has given us such wonders as television, space rockets, hydrogen bombs, napalm, twenty-four-hour deodorants, and the Pill.

Where would we be today without science? Where will we be tomorrow with it?

AFTERTHOUGHT:

The teaching of science has been greatly advanced by the use of television. The watcher of television receives graphic instruction in anatomy, learning about the intricacies of the nasal passages, the cough control mechanism, and the intestinal tract. He also receives instruction in the protein content of breakfast foods and the chemistry of gasoline additives. And just think what can be learned by a student with an interdisciplinary major in physics and chemistry who watches complicated experiments being made with a powerful new denture. There is no reason why everyone should not be *au courant* in what, to mix languages, I have earlier called *Wissenschaft*.

I confess that I wrote this article largely to impress a scientist friend of mine. The only trouble is that he is so busy with his technical journals that he seems never to have time to read my writings, such as this which appeared in *Playboy*, and he still thinks I know next to nothing about science. I had hoped he would notice the offhand way I dropped the names of Kirchhoff, Hittorf, Boltsmann, and Hasenöhrl. Then again, perhaps I am lucky. He might have asked me something about them.

And Make It a Sonnet, if You Don't Mind

At autograph parties, I try to do a little more than scribble my signature. I may, for instance, ask the young lady who wants the book autographed what her name is. This enables me to write "For Catherine, with best regards."

Not until I have written this and handed her the book does she tell me her name is spelled Kathryn.

What do I do then? I have several alternatives:

1. I cross out "Catherine" and write "Kathryn" above it. This is the easiest way, and it makes one thing very certain: the young lady will never again buy a book of mine.

2. With skill developed by much practice, I turn the name "Catherine" into "Kathryn." The "ath" requires no change, being in both names. Making a "C" into a "K" is not for beginners, and takes all of my artistry.

But where I have real trouble is making a "y" out of the "i," especially getting rid of the dot. Sometimes I extend the dot into a line, making it look as if my hand is a little unsteady. Then again, I may add a second dot, giving the effect of an umlaut. Whatever I do, it's a botch.

3. Using a razor blade I carry for just such emergencies, I remove the page on which I have written and autograph another page. Unfortunately, I sometimes have autographed the title page, removal of which is rather noticeable.

4. Looking appealingly at the bookstore manager, I suggest that he let me have a fresh copy. He can then tear out the "Catherine" page and return the book to the publisher as a damaged copy. This seems to me not asking very much, but bookstore managers never appear happy about such a logical solution.

The safest thing to do, I have found, is to ask the purchaser to write (print) his or her name so that I shall not make any error. This is so obvious and sensible that I almost never remember to do it.

Once, after autographing a book, I found that the jacket had been put on upside down. At first I tried to laugh it off (the situation, not the jacket), but the laugh was forced and the book purchaser did not join in. Then a thought came to me. After the upside-down autograph I wrote: "For the only person for whom I would autograph a book standing on my head."

But you can't get away with this sort of thing more than once. Ever since that narrow escape I have checked to see whether the jacket was upside down, and the book therefore downside up, before writing anything.

Frequently, all too frequently, the customer says, as I poise my pen over the page, "Write something clever." Once I did just that. I wrote: "Something clever." This lost me another friend, a friend being anyone who, having bought one of my books, buys another.

One little trick I have learned, after twice failing to catch the person's last name, and being embarrassed to ask a third time, is to say, "How about my using just your first name? It will be more personal that way." Usually this works, unless by that time I have remembered the last name but can't think of the first.

Book purchasers are always delighted with an inscription that is personal or familiar. For instance, they like me to write "With love" instead of "With best regards." Once, though, I got into trouble by sounding familiar when I really didn't mean to. A very attractive young wife, in a Southern city, met me at the airport and drove me to my lecture engagement. Later she drove me to the bookstore where I was having an autograph party. She bought a book of mine and asked me to autograph it. Wishing to express my appreciation for her helpfulness, I wrote: "For ———, who transported me." Sensing that someone might misinterpret this (she was really a looker, and I confess I had been looking), I added a few words, making it "who transported me in her car." Later I heard that her husband, a Southern gentlemen of the old school, gave his wife a bad time.

"I suppose you parked up on Honeysuckle Drive," he snarled, "with that author friend of yours."

Sometimes I am asked not only to write something clever but to write in verse. With the book purchaser looking over my shoulder, and with no chance for either a trial run or revision, I do my best. So far I have been getting away with a simple a-a-b-b quatrain. One of these days, though, I confidently expect someone to say, "And make it a sonnet, if you don't mind. I love sonnets."

I might be able to stall a little, meanwhile working out the rhyme scheme on a memo pad, by asking, "Which sonnet form would you prefer, Shakespearean or Petrarchan?"

I usually write an inscription slantwise across the page.

That way it looks more literary, somehow, and a few words will cover more space. Extra-large handwriting, with a few spectacular flourishes, has the same effect. There have been times, however, when I have written so large and with such a slant that when I finished my inscription I was down in the lower right-hand corner with no room for my signature. If you have ever painted yourself into a corner, you will know what it feels like. But you may not have had someone standing over you, watching you do it and wondering how you are going to get out of it.

When I get caught this way, I have no pat solution. If there is room, I write my initials instead of my full signature and explain, "It's more personal that way," as if this was what I had intended all along. Or, though I haven't anything more to say, I turn over the page and write another sentence or two before concluding with my signature. Again, I try to be nonchalant about it, as if this is what I had had in mind from the start. "You inspire me," I say to the beaming book purchaser.

I like to autograph with my own pen. Now and then a lady will hand me her pen when I am looking around for mine, and it turns out to write with red ink, or green. Red ink gives the impression that I have dipped the pen in a vein or, if it is a broad-point pen, an artery. Green ink makes me look sick, or makes me sick when I look at it.

Occasionally when someone has offered me a pen, and I have used it, I fail to return it. I do not do this on purpose, but it does keep me well stocked with pens, most of them better than the cheap ones I buy. My favorite pen is the one I picked up at an autograph party in Cleveland. I keep it on my desk, being afraid I might leave it behind at some bookstore.

I enjoy autographing books. I will autograph even a

sixty-cent paperback, the ten percent royalty on which is six cents. Not that I get six cents a copy, of course. After the original publisher takes fifty percent, the illustrator twenty percent, and my agent ten percent, I net two cents. Before taxes, that is. If I write a twenty-word inscription, that's one-tenth of a cent a word. It's a hard way to make a living.

Most people cherish an autographed copy of a book and wouldn't think of discarding it, even if they have no intention of reading it. But the other day I chanced upon a book of mine with an effusive, carefully wrought inscription. It was in a bookstore dealing in secondhand books. Autographed books, containing only the signature of an author like Ogden Nash or S. J. Perelman, were substantially marked up.

But my book, with that elaborate inscription, was in a special category. It was on a table with a sign: "Anything on this table fifty cents."

Was I downhearted? No. The person who should feel bad is the woman for whom I wrote the flattering, friendly inscription. Frankly, I can't remember who she is. And I'm glad of it.

AFTERTHOUGHT:

The greatest indignity to which an author is subjected occurs when people come to an autograph party and eat the cookies and drink the punch but don't even look at his book. They show their esteem for him, however, by asking for his autograph on a slip of paper or, sometimes, in a competitor's book. I am always worried about signing a slip of paper, especially for someone who looks like an artist. He might make the piece of paper into a reasonable facsimile of a blank check. Of course he would need to know the name of my bank. When anyone asks me, "Where do you bank?" while I am writing my name on a check-size slip of paper, I get a little suspicious. Fortunately, my hand starts shaking and my signature would never get by the teller.

Once a cute teenage girl for whom I was autographing a slip of paper made me feel very good for a moment, almost as good as if she had bought a book.

"I could trade your signature for Frank Sinatra's," she said, "but I won't."

"Oh, go ahead," I said, feeling magnanimous. I was in the big leagues, sure enough.

"No," she said, "I don't have enough of yours. It takes a hundred to get one Sinatra."

It was the first time I ever felt like a low-denomination trading stamp.

Oh, to Be Twenty-
Twenty Again

Benjamin Franklin, one of the most versatile Americans, was not only a Founding Father and Ambassador to France and the author of *Poor Richard's Almanac* and a famous kite flier but the inventor of bifocals. But for Ben, some of us might have to use two pairs of glasses, one for ordinary use and one for reading. With bifocals, we can see at a distance and up close with the same pair of specs, provided we have learned how to move our eyes up and down without getting them stuck in the middle.

Most people learn how to use bifocals in a few days, just as most people quickly become accustomed to dental plates. But I belong to that unhappy minority who can't quite get the hang of things or, for things that don't hang but perch, the fit of things. After twelve years, I still look out of the wrong part of my bifocals about half the time.

When I look up from reading, I lift my head instead of my eyes, and anything more than six feet away is a blur. And when I am reading, I often drop my head (many of the books I read these days are the kind that make me drop, or hang, my head) instead of my eyes, and the print almost disappears, right in an exciting part.

Some people tell me I should get trifocals, which were not invented by Benjamin Franklin. "I put them on in my optometrist's office," they tell me, "and walked right out, and never had the slightest bit of trouble." I could have put them on in the optometrist's office, too, and walked right out, but I would probably have groped my way along the hall and fallen down the steps.

My trouble, though, is not merely with bifocals, it is with glasses in general. In the first place, I dread a visit to the oculist almost as much as to the dentist. (I used the word *optometrist* a while back, and now have switched to *oculist*. I want to be equally unfair to both.) Not that there is any pain, any drilling into the eyeballs. What I dread is having to make difficult choices. Decisions have always been hard for me.

"Which looks better?" my man asks, then adds, "this one," as I look through a lens at a chart at the end of the long, narrow room, "or," when he has slipped in another lens, "this one?" Frankly, they look exactly the same to me, but I have to say something, not to disappoint him. "The first one," I say, trying to sound positive, though my heart isn't in it. This goes on for about half an hour, and since I am faced with decision after decision, I am in agony.

Even worse than selecting the right (or right and left) lenses is selecting the frames.

"These are the very latest," he says, putting on some frames with heavy black rims and with bows that slip straight back against the side of my head and would be wide enough to contain a hearing aid if I needed one.

"I don't know," I say. "Haven't you something a little less conspicuous?" What I really want are glasses that don't show at all, and yet are sturdy enough not to break, even when I accidentally sit on them, as I did with my last pair. I have already learned, after a painful experience, that my eyeballs are the wrong shape, or something, to permit me to wear contacts. Now I hate everyone with the right kind of eyeballs.

After trying on glasses with steel rims and with no rims, round glasses and oblong glasses, I wind up with a pair exactly like my old glasses, to which I have grown accustomed. No sooner are they made up and delivered to me, however, than I see a friend wearing the new-style glasses. Suddenly I realize that mine are old-fashioned and that they make me look middle-aged, which I am. But I have worn the new glasses for three days and would take a loss, as I would with a new car that had been driven around the block, if I traded them in. So I stick with my choice, feeling terribly out of style and behind the times. The next time I have to change my glasses for stronger ones, which won't be long, the way my eyes are deteriorating, I swear I'll get some frames that are up-to-date and smart. But, secretly, I know I won't.

Of course my greatest trouble with glasses is not having them. The commonest cry, or wail, around our house is my "Have you seen my glasses?" My wife, who has probably also misplaced her glasses, is a poor person to ask. From years of squinting, to read small print without her glasses, or to look for her glasses or mine, her eyes have narrowed into slits. This gives her a rather Oriental look, which some consider exotic. There is another odd thing about my wife. Sometimes, even when she has her glasses and needs them, she doesn't use them, but squints instead. She's probably afraid of wearing out the lenses by looking through them too much.

The only article I misplace more than my glasses is my

glasses case. I have tried to train myself so that when I put on my glasses I automatically slip my glasses case into my inside coat pocket. But though I can train a dog, I am no good at training myself. It may be, of course, that the average dog is smarter. Also, just as I am getting fairly good at remembering to thrust my glasses case into my inside coat pocket (one time in four), I find myself not wearing a coat, and this throws me. Even worse, sometimes the reason I am not wearing a coat is that I have forgotten where I left it.

Once, not having on a coat, I meant to put my glasses case in my back pants pocket, but I got confused and put my glasses there instead. That was the time I sat on my glasses and broke them.

I have tried to free myself from slavery to glasses by doing some eye exercises I read about. Every day for several weeks I faithfully rolled my eyes—up as far as possible, down as far as possible, to the right and then to the left as far as possible—to strengthen the eye muscles. I was sitting in an airport waiting room one day, vigorously rolling my eyes, and when I stopped for a moment I found that a crowd had gathered.

"He's having a fit," I heard someone say.

"He's nuts," someone else remarked.

One woman nudged her husband. "You'd better telephone the psychiatric ward at the hospital," she said. "I'll stay here and watch."

She didn't say she would do anything else, such as help hold me down if I became violent. All she planned to do was watch. Apparently she got a kick out of my eyes rolling.

I made my getaway before the men in white jackets arrived. It was the last time I did my eye exercises, which weren't helping anyhow.

Now if I can just find my glasses case. . . .

AFTERTHOUGHT:

I have learned how to save time searching for my glasses case. In addition to my regular case, I have three spares that I keep in a desk drawer. Instead of looking all over for my glasses case, I take out one of the spares. When I misplace this, I take out another. About the time I am down to my last case, I find one of the cases I lost earlier in the day. There are times during the day when I have only one case and times when I have all four.

I am thinking of putting a blackboard over my desk and charting my highs and lows. It would be interesting to know, over a period of months, whether there is any pattern: whether the lows, for instance, come at certain hours of the day and certain days of the week. There might be some relationship to the room temperature, my pulse rate, my sex life, or the price of gold. My findings might well have far-reaching implications, and I should have no trouble getting a government grant for research. Who knows what might follow? Maybe a Nobel Prize.

Watch Out

I am not and never have been a bird-watcher. Of course I have now and then glanced at a bird sitting on a telephone wire or a fence post. Or I have noticed a bird flying through the air, flapping his (or her) wings and gliding and swooping, and have thought it must be fun.

But I cannot tell a thrush from a lark or an oriole from a sparrow, to mention just about all of the bird names I know—these having been picked up from reading poetry rather than from studying ornithology. "That's the wise thrush; he sings each song twice over," wrote Browning, who seemed to like repetition. "Lo! here the gentle lark," exclaimed Shakespeare, though I have always thought "here" a textual error that should be corrected to "hear." Emily Dickinson sang of "the blissful oriole," perhaps because it had a mate, while she did not. And Edna St. Vincent Millay, another of our great women poets, has given us the fascinating line, "Lesbia with her sparrow," that taxes my imagination.

You may ascribe my not being a bird-watcher to lack of interest in birds, laziness, or just plain orneriness. (And I have looked up orneriness and found it is not, as I had hoped, related to ornithology.) The reason I am not a bird-watcher is that, in this age of Big Brother and wiretapping, I do not wish to do to birds what others may, at this moment, be doing to me.

How would you like to have someone with binoculars and a notebook forever spying on you? How would you like such a person to cry out excitedly, "Look! A bald-headed, crimson-breasted homunculus." The crimson-breasted might be only because you are wearing a crimson tie, perhaps to let everyone know you went to Harvard. How would you like a whole crowd of watchers, alerted by this cry, to train their binoculars upon you? What happened to Peeping Tom should happen to them, though Tom got more of an eyeful, even without binoculars, before being punished for his inquisitiveness.

Unpleasant though it would be to be watched this closely by people, I am still more uneasy at the thought of bird people-watchers. I can imagine a vulture suddenly swooping down upon me as I am working in my garden. The vulture would not have in mind any premature nibbling but only getting a closer look at this rare specimen, one of the last of a vanishing species. I can also imagine a hummingbird hovering within inches of me, staring through its tiny binoculars and meanwhile humming and maybe also hawing at such a strange sight.

I would find it embarrassing. I would consider it invasion of privacy. I would report it to the authorities, by which I mean either the police or authorities on bird life, such as members of the Audubon Society. If no action were taken, I would be forced to protect myself, perhaps with a BB gun.

Bird-watchers of the world, be careful. Just as we have developed nuclear weapons, so also birds may be working in secret, may be near a breakthrough, may soon have bird-size nuclear bombs themselves.

What birds can now drop, with uncanny accuracy, is nothing to what they may someday drop on those who persist in prying into their personal affairs. My suggestion to bird-watchers is to quit while there is still time. If you have to be doing something, take up astronomy. The stars are less likely to object to your watching, provided you keep your distance.

AFTERTHOUGHT:

As I have said, most of what I know about birds I have learned from the poets. The bird most written about, and therefore the one I know best, is the lark. Someday I think I shall collect an anthology of poems about the lark, and in a critical introduction, critical of both birds and poets, try to explain why poets find the lark so appealing.

In general, poets seem to like the noisier birds, and I gather from Shelley that the lark, or at least the skylark, sings even as it soars, losing not a moment. Of course, Shelley is a little confusing, or confused, for at one point he categorically denies that the skylark is a bird. "Bird thou never wert," he says, in a line that curls the hair of ornithologists, who classify the skylark as the Old World lark, commonly known as *Alauda arvensis.* Later in his poem, however, Shelley retreats a bit from his flat statement and says it might be a "sprite *or* bird." If I were writing a poem about a skylark, I would tell some of the things Shelley probably knew but would have found it embarrassing to mention, such as the fact that the male and the female take turns sitting on the eggs. That, it seems to me, is the stuff of poetry, especially lyrics.

Next to the lark, I should say that the most popular bird with poets is the nightingale. It, also, is a tireless singer, keeping at it far into the night. As Chaucer says, when writing of the young Squire:

> So hoote he lovede that by nyghtertale
> He sleep namoore than dooth a nyghtyngale.

Apparently the nightingale, troubled by insomnia, sings to while away the lonely hours. What Chaucer fails to point out is that the nightingale is inconsiderate of those who, but for his incessant warbling, might get a good night's sleep.

One of the most famous poems about this bird is Keats's *Ode to a Nightingale,* which some believe was written because the poet had run out of reasonable subjects, such as melancholy, autumn, and Grecian urns. Be that as it may, Keats said to the nightingale, which may not even have heard him, that he was about to take off and join him. "I will fly to thee," Keats promised, or threatened. How did he plan to make the flight? On what he called "the viewless wings of Poesy," apparently wings that were not only retractable but invisible.

There seems to have been a problem of aerodynamics. Whatever the reason, Keats never made it. Had he done so, however, soaring around with the nightingale and no doubt joining him in song, he would have beaten the Wright brothers by eighty-four years. And Orville and Wilbur stayed up only twelve seconds, while Keats, a very determined young man, would have flapped around with that nightingale until morning.

Something to Worry About

My friends are forever just leaving for, or returning from, some distant and exotic place. Increasingly they try to go where no one else in their social circle has been, and increasingly this is getting hard to do.

But the important thing to me is that my friends usually bring me "a little something" from a far-off place. They do this either out of compassion for me, the stay-at-home, or (and I think this more likely) to prove they were wherever they say they have been.

Recently a friend of mine brought me a string of worry beads. He had picked them up in Istanbul, along with the fez he was wearing and the odd shoes with turned-up toes in which he was walking with some difficulty. There could be no doubt that he had been in Turkey and shopped in the bazaars.

"You can use them instead of smoking," he said, handing me the beads. "They won't give you lung cancer."

"Thank you," I said. "Very thoughtful of you." I hoped he had washed them. I might not get lung cancer, but I might contract some horrible skin disease.

"And you can fiddle with them instead of chewing gum or cracking your knuckles or biting your fingernails," he added helpfully.

"Just what I've always wanted," I said, trying to stop cracking a knuckle that was only half cracked. "Is there any special way to use them?"

"When you're angry," he said, "you just hold them in your hand, gripping them tightly until you get control of yourself. Or if you have a problem to solve, you push the beads around, one at a time. It helps you think."

"Anything else?" I asked, dangling the string of beads and beginning to work with them.

"You can slip the beads over your wrist and wear them like a bracelet. This will draw attention to you if you are at a party and feel left out."

"Good," I said. "But won't I be thought—well—a little odd, wearing a bead bracelet?"

"That's a chance you have to take," he said. "But it's better than worrying, isn't it?"

So my friend left me with the worry beads. He was carrying a string himself, fingering them as he walked away. He didn't seem to have a care in the world, except to keep from tripping himself up in those Turkish shoes.

I examined the beads more carefully. They were a yellowish color, and highly polished. For a moment I thought, knowing my friend, that they might be second-hand, the polish resulting from much fondling by sweaty palms. There were fifteen beads, threaded loosely on a string and easy to move about. A large bead held the two ends of the string, and tied to it was a small tassel, rather gay and sporty looking.

My friend had, indeed, brought me an appropriate gift. I am a worrier. I worry about war and the stock market and earthquakes and, especially, about myself. I always expect the worst, and am rarely disappointed.

I even worry about worrying, since I am told it causes high blood pressure. But now that I had a string of worry beads, everything was going to be different.

The first time anyone saw me using my worry beads, I was sitting at a lunch counter. Fingering my beads for all I was worth, I rubbed each bead for a few seconds and then let it drop down the string. You see, I had a special reason to worry. I had foolishly eaten a crab salad. I like crab, but, as the saying goes, crab doesn't like me. If I got sick, as I always did, it would be in about thirty minutes, at one o'clock, and that was when I had made an appointment. . . .

Bill Whitmore, the fellow who sells me my life insurance, was sitting at the lunch counter two stools from me, and leaning over and looking at me quizzically. That crab must be getting to work already, I thought, and I'm looking pale, and Bill thinks his company may have to pay up on that policy sooner than the actuarial tables indicate.

"Hi," he said, lifting his fork in a friendly gesture.

"Hi, Bill," I said as heartily as I could, not wishing him to be too concerned about me. I might look a little under the weather, but not that far under.

"I didn't know you were a Catholic," he said, nodding toward my beads.

"I'm not," I said. "I'm a Congregationalist. These are worry beads."

"Oh," he said, and went back to eating. But I could see I had him worried, or at least confused, and thought of sliding the beads down the counter to him, to help him out. But he asked for his bill and left in a hurry, most of his lunch uneaten.

The next time my worry beads upset anyone was when I was getting gasoline at the service station on the corner.

"Fill 'er up with the premium," I said, feeling like a big spender. The attendant opened the gas tank, stuck in the nozzle of the hose, pulled a lever, and the little figures showing gallons of gasoline and numbers of dollars started whirring around.

I got out my worry beads. About the time the gauge showed $3.86, I began to finger the beads. Maybe I could have got by with the regular, I thought, or half and half. I probably shouldn't have filled the tank. The gas will slop out or evaporate. If I'm in a head-on collision, there will be more gasoline to explode and catch fire. Besides, there may be another gas war any day. It looks as if I'm getting only about twelve miles to the gallon. This car is a lemon. . . .

The service station attendant, who had been cleaning my windshield, was looking at me through a round place he had wiped dry. He seemed spellbound, watching my hands.

"These are worry beads," I said, holding them up so he could see.

"You must be the nervous type," he said.

"Not really," I said, though I was getting a bit edgy as he kept staring through that clean spot in the windshield, straight at me. "Anyhow, I don't smoke or chew gum or crack my knuckles or bite my fingernails."

"Is that a fact?" he said. I could see he thought I was missing a lot of fun.

"Would you mind finishing that windshield?" I asked. "I've got to be going."

"O.K.," he said, but he kept watching me as he carefully scraped off a couple of bug smears that were really too small to bother with. By the time I paid up and drove off, one hand on the steering wheel and the other working away at the worry beads, I had a bad case of the fidgets.

I might have kept on using my worry beads, except for an unfortunate occurrence. One day, while I was waiting in line at the teller's window of our local bank, worried about the balance in my checking account and annoyed at having chosen the slowest-moving line, I tugged away a little harder than usual at my worry beads.

Just as I reached the teller's window, it happened. The string holding the beads broke, and the beads rolled helter-skelter over the floor.

I didn't mind getting down on my hands and knees, looking for beads. I didn't mind one or two beads getting stepped on, and crushed, by people behind me. I didn't even mind having a big bruiser pick up one of the beads and call out, "Which one of you ladies lost this?"

What I hated was losing my place in line.

I never got my worry beads restrung. I just put the beads in my desk drawer, loose. Every time I pull out the drawer, the beads roll around and make a noise that sets my nerves on edge.

But it beats carrying them.

AFTERTHOUGHT:

I continue to be a worrier, with or without worry beads. In fact I sometimes even worry that I am not worrying, fearful that I may be overlooking something, or taking life too lightly.

One thing that worries me is that a dog is said to worry a bone. I should think a bone would worry a dog, especially if there happened to be very little meat on it or it was too tough for his teeth. However, I looked up the word "worry" the other day, when I was worried about not doing anything to improve my mind, and discovered that "worry" comes from the Anglo-Saxon word meaning "to strangle." Now I worry lest the dog worrying the bone swallow it the wrong way and strangle to death.

I worry because there is so much I don't know, and I worry because of some of the things I know. But I really don't need any worry beads. I have plenty of buttons I can twist off. And I have a novel way of biting my knuckles and cracking my fingernails.

A Short Dissertation
on Lips

I have been making a study of the female lip. A study in depth, you might call it, though I am more concerned with the exterior of the lip than with all the blood vessels, nerves, muscles, and whatnot underneath.

What started me thinking, I suppose, was that lower lip of Sophia Loren's. It is what is called a full lower lip. The other kind is simply called a lower lip, not an empty lower lip. What a full lower lip is full of is a rather personal matter, and I would just as soon not go into it. I had a great-grandmother from Kentucky, and I know what her lower lip was full of. Snuff. But Sophia Loren isn't from Kentucky, she's from Italy, and her lower lip is full of something else. Maybe honey.

That full lower lip of Sophia Loren's is an amazing thing. It has a curious sensual appeal. It gives you the feeling that she is pouting because no one has kissed her for the last few minutes. You have a great urge to plant a kiss on that marvelous lip yourself, rather than keep her waiting any longer, and you are just about to step up and do it when you recognize from the pictures you have seen that the man standing next to her is her husband. That lip is his. That is, it is Sophia's but he has charge of it.

Back in the twenties and thirties, the great sex queens of the movies, like Clara Bow and Jean Harlow, had tiny Cupid's bow lips. Their tongue, I guess, was the arrow. Sometimes a screen star looked as though she had just eaten a green persimmon. What was attractive about her lips was that they looked all puckered up and ready. But they rather monotonously stayed puckered all the time, even when their owner was screaming for help, forced to do something she insisted she didn't want to do, even as she was doing it, such as getting into an automobile with a stranger.

Until Marilyn Monroe came along, a woman with her mouth always slightly open and her lips quivering probably had adenoids and a nervous tic. But Marilyn Monroe made parted lips popular. If they glistened a little, as if covered by nail polish, so much the better. Imitating Marilyn Monroe, starlets went around with their mouths slightly open and their lips quivering. They may not have done it as well as Marilyn, but they gave a man the general effect. The general effect was helplessness and willingness, tinged with imbecility.

When I was in high school I knew a girl who had upside-down lips, or at least so they appeared. That is, her upper lip was where her lower lip should have been and her lower lip was where her upper lip should have been. She was pretty, in a freakish sort of way, and stood out in a crowd. They say this sort of thing happens only once in 100,000,000, so I was a lucky fellow, really privileged to get in on it.

Of course, all of us boys wanted to know how it felt to kiss a girl with upside-down lips, and we had our chance. At the senior-class party there was a booth where kisses were for sale, and this girl was on duty for about an hour. She made a killing. I guess there's nothing like doing something different, or doing the same old thing in a different way. I kissed her three times, at fifty cents each, and could have done it again if I had had the money, but $1.50 was all I had on me. There was something special about it, something once in a lifetime. You had the curious feeling of kissing a girl who was standing on her head and yet her face was up at the usual place. It could be that this is what started my interest in lips, even before Sophia Loren.

In college there was a girl who was said to have the hottest lips in our class. When she was kissed, she gave off sparks, or maybe it only seemed that way. There was a rumor that she sprinkled her lips with cayenne pepper. Certainly there was a distinct aftertaste, though to me it was a little more like spearmint. Her upper teeth stuck out a little, but instead of getting in the way or being uncomfortable, they gave you an extra thrill. There was a kind of intensity and purposefulness about her kissing that was possible only with teeth like that. They scraped your own teeth a little and made a tingling go up and down your spine and there was something really intimate about the whole business.

But this is not about teeth, it's about lips. The word "lip" goes back through Middle English to the Anglo-Saxon *lippa* and is related to the Latin *labium*. More interesting, or more discussible, is the theory held by some philologists that "lip" has some connection with "lap." Just how one's lip is connected with one's lap is something for the student of anatomy to look into. It may be connected, but there is quite an area in between. Fortunately, there is not an upper lap and a lower lap.

This gives rise to an interesting speculation. What if you had only one lip? And what if you had a choice and could have either an upper lip or a lower lip, but not both? I know which of Sophia Loren's lips I would rather have, even for only a few minutes. As for Elizabeth Taylor, whose lips I have been studying with some thoroughness lately, the upper and lower are equally good, and it would be agonizing to have to make a choice. The time I like Elizabeth Taylor's lips best is when they are pressed tightly against Richard Burton's. They may look all flattened out and squashed, but since I always identify perfectly with Burton, I am having such a good time I don't notice.

This suggests that it isn't so much how a woman's lips look as how they feel. If they are smooth and resilient, it doesn't matter what shape they are. They should give, but they should also bounce right back and not remain flat. They should also be warm. A good temperature, I have found, is 98.6 degrees. Whether they should also be moist is a matter of taste.

As long ago as the ancient Egyptians, women colored their lips so that men would notice they had them. At first they used things like overripe berries, and berries could be a nuisance and were hard to carry around in a handbag, where they could make a mess if they got smashed. The coming of lipstick made it possible to stand in front of a mirror, putting on lipstick, for hours, for the sole purpose of being late. When a woman puts on lipstick, she first rubs the lipstick all over her lips and then does a finish job with her finger, around the edges. Then she purses her lips until they completely disappear and then pops them out again. Then she rubs her upper lip with her lower lip until she has got rid of most of the lipstick. Then she starts applying her lipstick all over again.

Until recently, women colored their lips red, either because they thought that would be the color of their lips if they were healthy, normal women or because they thought that was the color men liked women's lips to be. Now they color them to match their eyes, which may or may not be red, or their dress or their draperies or the upholstery of their car. This leads to some interesting shades of blue, green, and purple. There is also a kind of gray lipstick that makes the lips look as if they were chapped or, in some instances, not there at all. This causes men to stare, wondering, "Where are her lips?" and once a man has started to stare, he may see something else he likes and be hooked.

When lips have been completely obliterated, the next step is obvious. Women will draw, or perhaps have tattooed, another pair of lips in an unusual place, as a conversation piece. Maybe on their cheek, or on their forehead, or on the back of their neck, or any old place. They may even have several pairs of lips, and a man who is trying to steal a kiss will, understandably, be confused.

"Where are the real ones?" he will pant, pretty wrought up after several false starts.

"Keep trying," she will say. "Faint heart ne'er won fair lips."

When you analyze them, there is nothing really beautiful about those two strips of flesh known as a woman's lips. But usually you don't analyze them. You feel rather than think, and when you feel, they feel good and so do you. The poets have hymned women's lips in many a deathless line. Take Shakespeare's "And steal immortal blessing from her lips." Or Christopher Marlowe's "Her lips suck forth my soul." Or Suckling's description, which brings me back to Sophia Loren:

> Her lips were red, and one was thin,
> Compar'd to that was next her chin,
> Some bee had stung it newly.

This is a far cry from the scientific description of lips: "Fleshy or muscular parts composing the opening of the mouth in man and many other animals, and covering the teeth." The man who wrote that ought to get out of the laboratory, or hire a more attractive assistant.

Whatever their size or shape or color, women's lips are going to be around a long time. If you haven't had any contact with them lately, you are missing something.

AFTERTHOUGHT:

In writing about lips, it was inevitable that I should mention kissing. After all, kissing is the chief function of lips, except for keeping your mouth closed while you are eating, and for making certain sounds. (Just try to pronounce the letter "p" without using your lips.) I read somewhere that kissing began with primitive man's search for salt. After trying all sorts of places, he found the heaviest deposit on women's lips. Women rather enjoyed the sensation of being desalinized, and while being kissed would murmur ecstatically, "Take it off. Take it *all* off." Today, however, a problem is posed for the man who enjoys kissing but has been told by his doctor to go on a salt-free diet.

Life, I long ago discovered, is made up of difficult choices.

Booked for Bed

One of my greatest pleasures in life is reading in bed. Often I go to bed an hour or so early in order to have plenty of time to read. As the result of many years of experience, I have some suggestions to pass along to those who contemplate taking up this delightful pastime. They are as follows:

1. Choose your bed carefully. A double bed is better than a single bed, since it provides more room for books and other supplies, unless your wife is also in it and she wants to go to sleep and can't go to sleep when your light is on. (If she wears a black mask over her eyes to keep out the light, *you* can't go to sleep when you have finished reading, since you have the uneasy feeling that you are in bed with a burglar.) A king-size bed is even better, unless it makes you feel so kingly you are unable to concentrate on your reading because of problems of state.

2. Have a plentiful supply of pillows to prop yourself up with. Since four is a good number, you should have

five, because you must count on one always sliding off onto the floor. Bed rests are a help, with backs and arms and all the other features of a chair except legs. But they take the pleasure out of reading because (1) you feel you are cheating and get a guilt complex, and (2) you might as well get out of bed and sit in a chair and be really comfortable.

3. Take an ample stock of food and drink to bed with you. You may get started on a book like *The Decline and Fall of the Roman Empire,* in six volumes, and not be able to stop, and be in bed for a long time. Besides, there is something about reading in bed that gives you a starved feeling before you turn the first page. Some people have solved the problem by installing a refrigerator next to their bed. Others, equally ingenious, keep their bed in the kitchen.

4. The chief problem about eating in bed is crumbs. Bread crumbs are easier to remove than cracker crumbs, which break into smaller and smaller crumbs as you pick them up. You start out picking up one crumb and wind up with ten. As for bread, whole wheat is preferable to white bread, since the crumbs are easier to spot on white sheets. Pumpernickel is even better. This, of course, is assuming you wish to pick up the crumbs instead of pretending they are not there. One way to pick up crumbs is to smear butter and jam on a piece of bread and then place the bread, jam side down, on the sheet. Crumbs will stick to the jam and come up easily.

5. Drinking in bed presents something of a problem. Unless you sit up quite straight, it is almost impossible to drain the last few swallows from a glass. Usually when you have lifted your glass high enough, with your chin still down, the liquid sloshes over your chest and into the bedclothes. Reading is interrupted for half an hour while you change pajamas and sheets. Since coffee is inclined to

stain, while alcohol evaporates rapidly, many readers in bed have learned to stick to gin or vodka. Whiskey, I am sorry to report, leaves an ugly color.

6. Be careful in your selection of reading material. Nonfiction is better than fiction, because you won't fall asleep without learning how the story comes out. Of course reading very modern, current books in bed keeps some people awake, as they lie there tense and upset, thinking things like "What trash!" and "Aren't there any good books any more?" But even these worriers finally get to sleep if they take a couple of aspirin and try to read a book of poems.

7. Most people fall asleep with their light on and a book in their hands. The cost of burning a 100-watt light through the night is negligible. But anyone who has slept eight hours with his thumb clamped in a book will not soon forget the experience.

Now if you still plan to read in bed, good luck. And don't forget to keep handy an extra pair of reading glasses. The pair you drop off and roll over on will have had it.

AFTERTHOUGHT:

Once I attended the funeral of a friend and heard the preacher speak some words about the dear departed that I have never forgotten. This preacher had hurried to the home of my deceased friend and examined the books on his bedside table. They were the Bible and certain inspiring works of literature, such as Shakespeare's *Complete Plays,* Browning's *Poems,* and *Pilgrim's Progress.* Having carefully studied the passages underlined and the pages most worn, the preacher delivered a moving sermon on the character—and a lofty character it was—of my friend.

I was restless and uncomfortable throughout the service, thinking of the books and magazines on my own bed-side table. I could hardly wait to get home and make a few substitutions. But I swore I would drive cautiously, taking no chances on having a preacher make a post-mortem survey and deliver a sermon on *my* character. If, however, a few hints of his discoveries were leaked to the press, my otherwise poorly attended funeral might draw a crowd.

My Hong Kong Tailor
Is Better than Your
Hong Kong Tailor

Thanks largely to inheritance, since I do very little about either diet or exercise, I am a perfect 39. I can go into a clothing store and take a 39 Regular off the rack and walk right out in it. Of course I have to pay for it first. And I always ask that cuffs be put on my trousers, though if I were really in a hurry I could just fold the ends over a bit and, as I say, walk right out.

Of course no two human figures are exactly alike, any more than two sets of fingerprints are. So I admit to a couple of small deviations from the norm—not enough to be bothersome, but just enough to give me a pleasant individuality. My right shoulder is a trifle lower than my left, and I have what is commonly known as a swayback, though I prefer the medical and rather aristocratic-sounding term for it, lordosis. However, neither of these minor variations keeps me from being a perfect, or just about perfect, 39.

So it made no sense for me to get a suit tailored in Hong Kong, except that I was there and it was the thing to do. Besides, as soon as my friends heard I was going to Hong Kong they said I must go to their tailor. Those who hadn't been to Hong Kong knew somebody who was just back from there and had the name of someone. Maybe they even had one of his cards.

"You *must* go to Ching Lo," one of my friends told me. "He has wonderful English woolens. Feel this," he said, offering me the sleeve of his sports jacket. "I had it made three years ago. Wears like iron."

I felt the material, since he insisted, and could tell from the way it scraped the skin off my thumb and fore-finger that the reason it wore like iron was that it really was iron.

"It ought to last you for years," I said, since he was ob-viously waiting for a compliment and I couldn't force myself to say anything nice about the color or the pattern. Besides, my thumb was throbbing.

"What do you think I paid for it?" he asked, and my first guess, since I had heard how cheap clothes are in Hong Kong, was twenty dollars.

"Fifty dollars," I said, not wishing to rob him of his fun.

"Thirty dollars," he said triumphantly, and I was glad I had not mentioned the first figure that had popped into my head.

Another friend had a different tailor to suggest. "Go to Charlie Lam," he said. "He's positively the best in Hong Kong. Superb tailoring. I'm wearing one of his suits now. Look at that lining, and the extra buttons, and my name embroidered over the inside pocket."

"Beautiful," I said, unable to keep my eyes off the shoulders, where the coat sleeves had come loose and were hanging by long white threads.

"How much do you think it cost?" he asked, as I knew he would.

"Fifty dollars," I said, wishing him to get as much satisfaction as my other friend.

His face fell, and so did his sleeves. "How did you guess?" he asked, and I could see he was terribly hurt. "Somebody must have told you." He walked away, his sleeves hanging dejectedly, without showing me either the secret coin pocket or the double zipper that had been sewn into his fly for no extra cost.

When I arrived in Hong Kong I had the names of fourteen tailors. They were listed alphabetically, from Ace Tailoring to Tom Wu, with helpful notes about each, such as "fabulous silks," "serves free beer," and "ask for Harry." I had heard how fast the tailors work in Hong Kong, and how they can turn out a suit, from first measurements to finished product, in twenty-four hours. Though I was going to be there six days, I thought I had better get started on a suit and not have anyone working under pressure. That way I would probably get a better job.

The moment I finished unpacking, I headed for Hankow Road, where most of my addresses were. I could do my sightseeing later. My idea was to drop in on several of the tailors who had been recommended, look over their goods and prices, and finally select the most promising tailor to turn out a suit. One suit was all I had in mind. I really didn't need any more, and I was right up to my forty-four pounds and wasn't going to pay any surcharge to the airline.

As I walked along Hankow Road, checking the names and numbers against my address book, a young Chinese stepped out from a doorway.

"Sir, may I help you?" he asked, in such English English that I was almost ashamed to let him hear my low-class Western American.

"I'm looking for Ho Chang, the tailor," I said. "I don't seem to find the number."

"It *is* a bit difficult, sir," he said, sounding like a Chinese Commander Whitehead. "I shall be glad to show you."

With that, he started down a narrow alley, and I followed. Nice young fellow, I thought. Maybe a civil servant, or a student in the university.

"Here we are," my guide said, pointing to the sign, "Ho Chang, Expert Gentleman's Tailor," over the doorway. Then, holding the door open and bowing slightly, "Won't you enter, sir?"

I went in, and my escort followed. Probably he wished to make sure I was safely in the hands of an English-speaking tailor before he left me.

I walked toward a counter, behind which bolts of cloth —tweeds, silks, woolens of all patterns and weights—were piled to the ceiling. The enormous stock of cloth so entranced me that I did not at first notice that my young Chinese was now standing behind the counter.

"Pardon me, sir," he said. "Permit me to introduce myself." He handed me a card, on which was tastefully printed: "Henry Lum, Manager, Ho Chang Tailoring Company, Ltd.

"Oh," I said, "I didn't know you worked here."

"I am not an ordinary worker, sir," he said, reaching over the counter and pointing to his card, "I am the manager. I suppose you are interested in having some suits tailored."

"Just one suit, Mr. Lum," I said. "I arrived in Hong Kong only today, and this is the first shop I have been in. I want to look around a little before I decide."

"Of course," he said. "And please call me Henry.

Everyone does. Now, before we start looking at materials, what would you like to drink? Scotch, bourbon, gin, vodka, beer? Anything you like, on the house."

At that moment a beautiful young Chinese girl in a Suzie Wong dress, the skirt split up to an enticing point about twelve inches above her knees, slithered through the beaded doorway from a back room. Smiling and bowing, she approached me, placed her delicate hands on my lapels, and started to remove my coat.

"Let her have your coat, sir," Henry said, noticing I was a bit uncertain. "I want to take your measurements, just in case you see something you like."

What I liked was the Chinese girl. If I was breathing a little hard, I was merely trying to inhale as much as I could of the delicate perfume that wafted from her as she helped me out of my coat. It was a fragrance suggesting some indefinable Oriental something that I wanted to define.

"And tell Li Mei what you would like to drink, sir," Henry said. "We can start looking at some materials while she serves you."

*   *   *   *   *

I will not say that Li Mei put anything insidious in my drink, except alcohol, which can be insidious enough. Nor am I certain whether I fell asleep and had a most remarkable dream while I sat at the counter, looking at materials, or actually went through the whole experience. Dream or reality, I have a blurred recollection of climbing hand in hand with Li Mei up a curious mountain, made of swatches of silk and wool, and stopping to rest in a teahouse where Li Mei served me tea that tasted strangely and pleasantly like bourbon, and stroked my brow with her delicately tapered fingers. While I lay on a deliciously soft mound of suit linings, she leaned over and pressed her lips against mine. I pulled her down to me, and the moon was darkened by clouds—clouds that looked for all the world as if they were made of thousands of shiny buttons. . . .

What I *am* sure of is that I didn't go to any of the other thirteen Hong Kong tailors on my list after that session at Ho Chang's with Henry and Li Mei. One reason I did not go to any of the other tailors was that when I got back to my hotel and happened to put my hand in my pocket, I found a receipt signed by Henry Lum, Manager, Ho Chang Tailoring Company, Ltd. It indicated that I had ordered, and paid for, two winter-weight suits, a silk suit, a tropical worsted suit, two sports jackets, and three pairs of slacks. Oh, yes, and a dozen shirts. I was carrying a necktie which, not being on the bill, Henry had apparently given me, out of gratitude for my large order or out of pity. I also discovered a small silk handkerchief, with the initials L. M. on it, that had a fragrance like the interior of the teahouse up on the side of that silk-and-wool mountain.

My tongue was a little thick, and my pad of traveler's checks was a little thin. But I would not have to buy another suit for twenty years, unless styles changed.

Six days should have been enough to see all the sights of Hong Kong. But I never saw Repulse Bay or the Tiger Balm Garden or any more of Hong Kong harbor than I could glimpse out of my hotel window at night. I spent all day, every day, at the Ho Chang Tailoring Company, in part to get fitted and in part, a large part, to renew my acquaintance with Li Mei. The fittings went slowly, because Henry had turned his attention to a big spender from St. Louis, and I had been taken over by a subordinate, a sinister-looking Chinese tailor who spoke no English and smelled of opium—or so I thought. I could have been wrong, since I had no idea what opium smelled like.

As for Li Mei, though Henry kept telling me she

would be back soon, I never saw her again. I wanted desperately to return her handkerchief to her. One day Henry said she was attending the funeral of a cousin. Another she was on a business trip for the firm. And still another she was home with a cold. Had I been of a suspicious nature, I would have thought she was avoiding me. Once, about closing time, I thought I saw her coming out of the back entrance with the man from St. Louis, who had his arm around her slender waist, but it was probably someone who looked like her.

The fittings were at last concluded, and I was told to pick up my four suits, two sports jackets, three pairs of slacks, and twelve shirts the next morning, which was the day before I was to leave Hong Kong. At the appointed hour I arrived at Ho Chang's to get my wardrobe.

"All ready for you," said Henry. He no longer used the "sir," in fact had dropped it the day my check was cleared.

"I'd like to try on one of the suit coats," I said, "just to be sure."

"There's no need to," Henry said, a bit brusquely.

"I know there's probably no need, and I'm sorry to bother you," I said apologetically. "But I'd hate to get all the way back to America and find something wrong."

"If you insist," Henry said. He handed one of the coats to me, as if he couldn't care less. "Go ahead, try it on." He looked at his watch. Apparently he had an appointment with the man from St. Louis.

I took off my old coat and slipped into the newly tailored one, with "Ho Chang Tailoring Company" on the inside pocket, and directly beneath it my name, embroidered in gold letters. It had cost me more than I had anticipated, in view of all I had heard about Hong Kong prices, but it was obviously a fine piece of tailoring.

"Oh, no!" I exclaimed, after a quick look into the three-sided mirror.

"Anything the matter?" Henry asked, idly curious but with no real concern in his voice.

"I'll say so," I said. "Look at these shoulders. One's a good two inches higher than the other."

"They look the same to me," Henry said. "It's your imagination."

"It's not my imagination," I said. "It's your tailor." I could see what had happened. The tailor had put the extra padding not in my low right shoulder but in my high left one. This, instead of leveling my shoulders, had made them doubly worse.

"I look like a freak," I said.

Henry said nothing, and I felt that for once he was agreeing.

"Get that tailor," I said sharply. "My plane takes off for Tokyo at one-thirty tomorrow and I leave the hotel at noon. You had better have this fixed by then. And the other coats, too, because I suppose the same error was made on all of them."

"I haven't admitted it was an error, sir," Henry said. The "sir" was back in, but after a pause and with an unpleasant emphasis. "It looks all right to me, but if you want that shoulder lowered, we'll lower it, and have it ready for you tomorrow morning. After all, it's your suit, and you have to wear it."

Henry was so sure of himself that I began to wonder. Maybe I was standing at an angle, or there was a bubble in the mirror, or something. But before taking the coat off and handing it to him, I looked at it very carefully again. Unless one of my eyeballs had dropped out of line, there was no question about it. The tailor had indeed padded the high shoulder, my left, and it was grotesquely higher than my right.

"Be sure you have the coats ready for me in the morning," I said. "I'll be in at ten. I leave for the airport at noon."

The next morning I was at Ho Chang's promptly at
10:00. I was packed and had paid my hotel bill.

"All finished and wrapped," Henry said when I came
into the shop.

"Maybe I'd better try on one coat if it isn't too much
trouble to unwrap it," I said. It was a sturdily wrapped
parcel, and I hated to have them undo it. But I wanted
to be absolutely sure.

Henry said something in Chinese. I don't know what it
was, but I didn't like the tone of it. Then he picked up a
large pair of scissors. From the look on his face, I thought
he was going to run me through, just above the belt
buckle. Instead, he savagely attacked the wrapping, not
bothering to cut the cord but ripping a hole through the
several layers of heavy paper.

"Here," he said gruffly, tossing a coat at me.

I slipped it on, just for a quick look. Horrors! At first
I forgot why I had put the coat on, and could see only
that I was monstrously deformed. Then I remembered.

"He's done it again!" I cried, half in anger and half in
frustration. The tailor, still mixed up, had piled two
more inches of padding onto that already hiked-up shoulder. Now it rose almost to my ear, while my right
shoulder drooped far below.

This time I had less trouble convincing Henry. He admitted that something was slightly amiss. In a last desperate effort to fasten the blame on me, he said that
maybe I had pointed to the wrong shoulder when looking
at the back of my coat in the three-way mirror, which
made everything opposite.

"I don't care whose fault it is," I said, "I just want
those shoulders made even. I don't want to look like
something in a side show. And I leave for the airport in
an hour and a half."

"Don't you worry," Henry said. "All we have to do is

pull all the padding out of that left shoulder and put a little into the right. You take your trousers and shirts. I'll send a boy down to the hotel with your coats as soon as they're ready."

I trusted him. There was nothing else I could do. But at five minutes of twelve, when I was in the airport limousine with all my luggage, there was no sign of the boy with my coats. At twelve, still no boy.

"Wait just a few minutes longer," I begged the driver. "This is very important to me." I could imagine myself back home with all those trousers and no coats. The other passengers in the limousine were looking at their watches and, none too pleasantly, at me.

At five minutes after twelve, just as the driver said he could wait no longer and pulled his door shut and started the motor, a boy came running up, burdened down by all the coats in his arms. Apparently there had been no time to wrap them, and I would have to carry them this way onto the plane. But I was happy to have them. We drove off, I buried under the pile of coats in my lap.

Once settled on the plane, and while others were reading magazines, I began to wonder how my coats would look now that the shoulders were even. I felt the left shoulder of one of the coats. There was no padding in it whatsoever. Now, at last, it must be even with the right. I thought I would try it on in the washroom.

Can you guess what I discovered? As I looked at myself in the narrow little mirror over the wash basin, I could see that the shoulders were, indeed, quite even. But that high left shoulder, the one that had been further raised, had had to be made larger in order to hold so much padding. Now, with the padding removed but otherwise no retailoring, the excess cloth hung over like an epaulet. . . .

I have never been able to get an American tailor to repair that left shoulder. Every time I have confronted a tailor with my problem, putting the coat on so he could see how ghastly it looked, the result has been the same. The tailor has had a good laugh, and then told me he wasn't interested in patching up a job someone else had bungled.

"But I'll pay you whatever you say," I begged one tailor, who had a kind look in his eyes.

"Some things you don't sell," he said. "Like pride in your profession."

"Then what shall I do?" I asked helplessly.

"Go back to Hong Kong," he said.

I was mistaken about that kind look in his eyes.

AFTERTHOUGHT:

I have been back to Hong Kong only once since that unhappy incident of the uneven shoulders. On my second visit, vowing to keep out of the clutches of tailors, I bought only an ivory letter opener that broke the first time I tried to open a letter with it. I had noticed the crack halfway across it but thought it looked rather nice, a sign of age and authenticity.

Why I wanted to look up the Ho Chang Tailoring Company, I don't know. But some atavistic impulse drew me there. It was no longer at its old location, and no one in any of the neighboring shops knew where it had moved to or, indeed, whether it was still in business. I doubt that it went bankrupt. More likely Henry Lum (who, I suspect, is also Ho Chang) retired after he cashed my check and is living on the Riviera—with Li Mei. It was fortunate for me that the tailor shop was not there. Had it been, I would probably have left my card, attached to a paving stone tossed through the plate-glass window. And I would now be doing time in a Hong Kong jail.

Though I have given up tailored suits, I have plenty of trouble with ready-mades. Natural-shoulder suits fail to compensate for that low right shoulder, and I look somewhat more lopsided than I did back in the days when padding was used more freely. But what makes it really hard for me to buy a new suit, aside from laying out all that money, is having to stand in front of a three-sided mirror. To borrow, and corrupt, a line out of *My Fair Lady,* "I've grown accustomed to my face." But I so rarely see my rear—swayback and all the rest—that the sight of it always comes to me as a shock. Between visits to a clothing store, growing ever more infrequent, I forget what I look like to people who see me from behind. Why must I be reminded, when I can't do anything about it?

If clothing stores are going to continue using three-sided mirrors, they might learn a lesson from cocktail bars: Keep the lights down very low. What you can't see won't hurt you.

Discovery of an
Unpublished Manuscript

Recently I bought an old medical book in a bookstore. I bought it not because of interest in the subject but because it was on a table that bore the sign: "Any book 50¢." It was a big, sturdy volume, and I thought it might suit my purpose. I needed something about two inches thick to put under a potted plant in our den.

It turned out to be just the right size, and the brown binding went rather nicely with the deep red of the flower pot. The only trouble was that the plant tilted slightly, no matter which way I turned it. It was then that I noticed several sheets of paper folded and tucked inside the back cover of the book. Once I had removed the wedge of paper, the plant stood up as straight as you please.

I was about to throw away the half-dozen sheets, which

were yellowed and worm-eaten around the edges, but something or other, it may have been the fastidious penmanship, caused me to read what appeared to be the manuscript of an article, or possibly the beginning of a book. It was entitled "Bedside Manners and Mannerisms, Being a Study of Certain Curious Categories of Physicians." The name of the author was illegible, since it had been so thoroughly erased that the paper was almost rubbed through, and only the suffixed "M.D." remained. Nor was the manuscript dated, though I could tell from two indisputable bits of internal evidence that the author must have lived many years ago. In the first place, there was that clear, careful penmanship, with no sign of haste and no effort made to mystify the patient or to make things difficult for the pharmacist. In the second place, references to visiting the home of the patient suggested that the writer lived in those early days when doctors still made house calls.

Skipping the writer's introductory remarks, which display a certain waspishness about his colleagues and make one understand why he erased his name, I come to the heart of the matter. Here are the various types of physicians as indicated by their bedside manner. I quote from the manuscript without changing a word:

1. *Ebullient*—This kind of physician is outgoing, even when he is coming in. He rings the doorbell vigorously and then enters with a virile, athletic stride. "I'm here!" he announces cheerily. Or, to identify himself and avoid being mistaken for the plumber or the meter reader, "It's me." (He knows it should be "It is I," but refuses to be stilted.) Laughing heartily, he bounds up the stairs (unless it is a one-story house) to the sickroom. If he has not heard or told a good joke all morning, which is unlikely, instead of laughing he may sing or whistle.

At the patient's bedside he begins the diagnosis with

some such penetrating question as, "Well, how are we feeling today?" This is not the royal "we" but the medical "we," intended to be reassuring. The patient and doctor are as one. What hurts one hurts the other, except that portion of the bill that is not covered by insurance.

Ebullient exudes good health, giving the patient hope that it is contagious. To keep in good health he plays golf Wednesdays, Saturdays, and Sundays. During the winter he uses a sunlamp. He bustles about the sickroom making cheering noises, perhaps rattling two bottles of pills as if they are gourds, or beating tempo with a tongue depressor. His purpose is to display confidence, cheerfulness, and *élan vital*. He vibrates with optimism and the power of positive thinking. He minimizes the illness, perhaps something trivial like gallstones, and assures the patient he will be up and about "in no time," which is rather soon.

When Ebullient, with a last slap on the patient's back, leaves the sickroom, laughing heartily over a parting joke, the patient is greatly encouraged. At last, he thinks, he can get a litle rest and quiet.

2. *Lugubrious*—The precise opposite of Ebullient is Lugubrious. He enters the sickroom as if he were an undertaker, come to remove the body. As he approaches the bed, on tiptoes, a pained look comes over his face. "Things don't look so good," he says, after feeling the patient's pulse with a cold, clammy hand. "You are feeling worse, aren't you?" he asks, nodding his head to encourage the patient to reply in the affirmative.

Lugubrious speaks in a low, sepulchral tone. Not only is there no cheerfulness in his voice, there is no hope. Though he may not say it to the patient, he will tell a relative in a loud whisper that the patient can overhear, "It's only a matter of time."

If, despite all prognostications, the patient recovers, Lugubrious will be none too happy about it. After all, who likes to be wrong? "Don't get your hopes too high," he says. "In such cases there is often a temporary turn for the better. But in the long run. . . ." He is of course absolutely right, if by the long run he means by the age of eighty or ninety.

When Lugubrious leaves the house, everyone but the patient breathes easier. The patient breathes harder, and is a little surprised to be breathing at all. Flowers by the bedside, only recently placed there, look wilted. It may only be his imagination.

3. *Fussbudget*—This type is a little like another type, the Happy Worrior, but keeps busier about it. He puts on surgical gloves before ringing the doorbell or touching the doorknob. He tests each stair carefully, to be sure it will bear his weight. Before approaching the patient, who has a fractured tibia, he dons a surgical mask to avoid contamination—not of the patient but of himself.

Fussbudget shakes down his clinical thermometer not a couple of times but until the mercury almost comes out the end. He wants to be sure it is well below normal before inserting it into his patient's mouth or rectum or wherever. He also carefully tests his stethoscope before use, placing it on his own chest and listening intently. Sometimes he becomes so preoccupied with what he hears that he forgets his patient entirely.

This physician insists on every possible test and a few that are impossible, taking samples of blood, saliva, skin, sperm, and anything else available. These he hand carries to the medical laboratory, anxiously sitting on a bench in the corridor until the tests have been completed. If all tests are negative, he feels somewhat reassured, but he is still not completely convinced. "Are you sure you ran them through properly?" he asks the laboratory technician. Then he scans the count on red corpuscles again, fearful that there may have been a typographical error.

Fussbudget keeps elaborate medical records, noting

such things as tendency to dandruff and the rate of toe-nail growth. Instead of one folder to a patient, he has a complete filing case drawer for each, and filing cases overflow into his bedroom. Before visiting a patient, he pores for hours over the records, especially on rainy days. (When it rains, he pores.) He hires a nurse not because of her looks, as other doctors do, but because she was valedictorian of her class at secretarial school.

Fussbudget leaves no stone unturned, except, eventually, the tombstone. He likes to be thought thorough, and thinks it a compliment when he overhears a colleague say, "He's a thorough ass." Once a patient fainted in his office. There was nothing much wrong with her except that she grew weak from lack of food while waiting for the doctor to complete his examination of the patient ahead of her.

4. *Speedy*—If Fussbudget takes too much time, Speedy helps average out. Speedy shakes the thermometer once, hard. He can count a pulse and look at a patient's tongue at the same time. Instead of sitting at the patient's bedside, he stands, thus saving the time of sitting down and getting up. He has a quick, staccato way of talking. "Whatsamatter?" he asks, or "Howd'yafeel?" When he prescribes, he says something terse, such as "Taketwo-aspirinasneeded." Pharmacists have a little trouble making out his prescriptions, because unlike other doctors he doesn't write illegibly. He uses shorthand.

Speedy is always looking at his watch. Indeed he has two watches, one on each wrist. One watch is a stopwatch. The other watch he thinks has stopped, but it really hasn't. It's just going at the normal speed, which he thinks frightfully slow. He is All Business. Some patients like him, because they think he is terribly efficient. Others think he is a little cold, like his stethoscope. Most see him such a short time that they really don't know what he is like. "You have changed," they say when he arrives the next day after his first visit, running up to the bed in his track shoes. But he hasn't actually changed. Patients get such a brief glimpse of him that they don't remember what he looked like before.

Ebullient, Lugubrious, Fussbudget, and Speedy are four of the types most commonly encountered. There are others, however, including. . . .

At this point the manuscript I found tucked into that medical book comes to an abrupt end. The last page is crumpled and torn. The large spot or stain at the bottom of the page, now almost faded out, could be ink—or blood. Did someone come upon the doctor as he was writing? Was there a violent struggle? Did someone else, not the writer, place the manuscript pages inside the medical book, where I found them many years later while straightening that flower pot? We shall never know what happened. However, it may well have been both the beginning and the end of a promising literary career.

I regret that the author of "Bedside Manners and Mannerisms" did not complete what might have been a classic work in the field of medical practice. By now, of course, it would be out of date, since the types described no longer exist. But it would be of interest to the medical historian and the collector of curiosa. And present-day physicians might be amused at the eccentric behavior of their predecessors.

AFTERTHOUGHT:

In *The Journal of the American Medical Association,* where this appeared, it is the custom to give the home address of the author and to suggest that requests for reprints be directed to him. Fortunately, the *Journal* gives the author a generous supply of reprints, though it would be still more fortunate if he were given a generous supply of postage stamps and time. This article on the various bedside manners brought requests for reprints from all over the world and made me for a moment feel like an M.D. instead of a lowly Ph.D. whom members of the family will not even trust to affix a Band-Aid. Of all the requests, I was most impressed by one from the Städtische Kliniken in Darmstadt. It was a printed form, though signed by Dr. med. Hans Richter, and what made me feel like a member of the worldwide medical fraternity was its being in three languages.

It began:

Sehr geehrter Herr
Monsieur et très honoré collègue! (I liked that collègue bit.)
Dear Sir! (Why, I wondered, was there no exclamation point after the German salutation? Are German doctors less given to emotion than their English and French colleagues?)

And then it went on:

Für die Übersendung eines Sonderdruckes Ihrer Arbeit wäre ich sehr dankbar.
Je vous serais très obligé de m'envoyer un tirage à part de votre article.
I should greatly appreciate to receive a reprint of your paper.

After profuse thanks it concluded, in German only (perhaps assuming that by now I was bilingual, if not trilingual):

Mit vorzüglicher Hochachtung.

Is it any wonder that I began prescribing cold cures to my neighbors with a new confidence, a new air of professionalism, occasionally lapsing into German or French?

Backward, Turn Backward

When I was in high school there was a fad that I wish we could bring back. It was more interesting than anything the young people today seem able to contrive, and I concede that today's young people are very inventive.

What we did, when I was in high school in the early twenties, was to call each other by our names spelled backward. I, for instance, was Drahcir Ruomra. I rather liked it. It had a romantic sound, a suggestion of Czech or Persian or anyhow the language of people more exotic than my own family, who had arrived from Scotland three generations before. The Ruomra slid off my tongue easily enough, but I had a little trouble with the Drahcir, not being sure whether to pronounce the "c" as a "k," an "s," or a "ch." At any rate, since I was unsure myself I didn't correct others.

My best friend was Rehpotsirhc Nospmoht. His first name was harder to say than mine, but since we had always called him Chris before, we settled for Sirhc, which wasn't so bad except for that "h." I think my girlfriend, Arabrab, had the prettiest first name in the class, and this helped, because she was only the third-prettiest girl. I would just as soon forget her last name, which was Skrap.

Though we never called him that to his face, among ourselves our principal was Mr. Terfmop, and it somehow seemed to fit him. On the other hand, we liked the name of our chemistry teacher, Mr. Swett, too much to change it to Ttews. Besides, we couldn't figure out how to pronounce those two "t's" unless we stuttered a little, which is what we would have done if necessary.

One way we got through American History, where our teacher was an old maid named Miss Retneprac, was to spell the names of the Presidents backward, starting with Egroeg Notgnihsaw and coming up to the President then in office, Nerraw Leilamag Gnidrah.

I was especially interested in President Gnidrah, because I visited Washington one summer with my parents and we managed to hook onto a party of visiting Elks and I shook his hand. "How do you do," President Gnidrah," I said, and he said, "Pleased to meet you," which was exactly what he said to the man in line just ahead of me. I had not intended to call him Gnidrah, but had got into the habit in that American History class and just couldn't help it. Fortunately, he didn't seem offended and may not even have heard me, because I was very small in those days and so was my voice.

Of all the presidents, I liked Klop best, but of course more for his name than for his achievements. I knew Maharba Nlocnil was the greatest, or at least our teacher said so. Actually I preferred the presidents with short names, such as Smada, Relyt, and Tfat. Tfat, Miss Retneprac told us, weighed 330 pounds, so if he wasn't our greatest President he was the biggest around and the best named. The hardest for me to handle was YelniKcM. That "KcM" threw me.

I wish Noxin had been President back in those days, with a Vice President named Orips Wenga.

AFTERTHOUGHT:

It was not until I got to college that I learned what a palindrome is. A palindrome, as you know, is a word or sentence that is the same when read backward or forward. A few examples are "madam," "Hannah," and what Napoleon is supposed to have said, though I doubt it: "Able was I ere I saw Elba." One I rather like, despite its cheating a little in the spelling of "dwell" as "dwel" and the use of an ampersand for "and," is "Lewd did I live, & evil I did dwel." I assume the comma has the same meaning, or effect, whether the tail turns to the left or to the right. At any rate the person who wrote it, if he (or she) was not just trying to write a clever palindrome, must have had an interesting life, perhaps as a peddler of pornography or pusher of drugs.

In this connection I must add that one of my greatest achievements was the discovery that "smut," spelled backward, is "Tums." Almost as interesting is the fact that "Tums" spelled backward is "smut."

The makers of Serutan advertise that the name of their product, spelled backward, is "Nature's." Perhaps I am a purist, as well as a person who usually gets along without a laxative, but how do they account for that apostrophe?

Let me stray from the subject of reading words backward long enough to tell you about my moonlighting as a writer of slogans for a rival laxative. After such a feeble attempt as "Flushed with Success," I wrote a slogan that brought me a letter of commendation from the Advertising Manager, though he said the advertising of laxatives is (or at least it was at that time) too delicate a business to use what I had written. This was my best (and last) effort: "It Takes the Toil out of Toilet."

Or, as I would have written it when I was in high school: "Ti Sekat eht Liot tuo fo Teliot."

Have You Ever Given
Much Thought to
a Paper Clip?

I have often wondered who invented the paper clip. It must have been someone with a knack for the simple solution of a simple or even a complex problem. The other name for such a person is a genius.

Of course, necessity is the mother of invention, and it may well be that the inventor was in desperate need of a device for doing what a paper clip does. Or, since many great inventions have been accidental, he may simply have been fiddling with a small piece of malleable wire when he made his Great Discovery.

We may never know the name of the inventor or the circumstances of this technological breakthrough. But we know the result: an ingenious little twist of wire that has done more for mankind than anything since the invention of the wheel.

It may have been a group effort, or the climax of an evolutionary process. But I like to think it the work of one man at a crucial moment of history, comparable to Edison and the electric light or Gillette and the safety razor.

From its name, it would seem that the function of a paper clip is to clip paper—not to cut it apart (as when one clips an advertisement or a coupon), but to hold pieces of paper together. This function it performs admirably, requiring only a little bending and adjusting occasionally in order to exert the maximum squeezing strength and holding power. But it is for its other uses that the paper clip has won our heartfelt gratitude.

A paper clip can be used as a bookmark, a tie clip, a money clip, and a hair curler. Uncoiled, and fully or partly straightened out, it is exactly right for scraping the bowl of a pipe, and not too bad for cleaning fingernails and picking teeth. Persons with a steady hand and a certain amount of courage use a paper clip for removing accumulated wax in the ear. Those even more highly skilled have been known to pick a lock, start a car, and fix a leaky toilet with this all-purpose tool.

A paper clip can usually be found in the repair kit of a television repairman, and in the little black bag of a physician, ready for any emergency.

I always keep a few paper clips in my coat pocket, along with toothpicks and antacid tablets. The only trouble with carrying more than one is that paper clips, like wire coat hangers, have a way of intertwining with one another.

Before a paper clip can be put to work, it must first be disentangled from one of its fellows, to which it clings desperately. I feel a little brutal about it, as if I am tearing apart a mother and child or two lovers. When I remember to do so, I carry several paper clips but keep them segregated, one to a pocket. This way, if time is of the essence there is no delay. I can bring a paper clip into action at once.

My own favorite use of a paper clip, when a safety pin is not available, is to clean my typewriter keys. Though it would help if the ends of the clip came to a sharp point, I can do a very good job on the "o" and the "p," and from years of practice I am fairly adept at the upper parts of the "e" and the "a." Only the "m" and the "w," with their narrow interstices, are too much for me. But I have written more fully about cleaning typewriter keys (one of my major obsessions) elsewhere. Forgive me if I keep returning to the subject.

The automobile has replaced the horse. The electric light has replaced the kerosene lamp. Nuclear power may replace coal and oil. But I see no sign of anything that will ever take the place of the paper clip. Its inventor will therefore be revered always as one of the movers and shakers of mankind, one of those who made life a little easier for us. If we knew his name, we could name something after him—such as a street or park or airport. Since we do not, I suggest another way to memorialize him.

Let us declare Paper Clip Day a national holiday. On that day we would all try to get along without a paper clip from morning till night. Papers would be scattered, wax would accumulate in ears, toilets would stick, typewriters would clog.

The next day we would be a little more grateful for the paper clip, and perhaps even say a little prayer for its inventor.

AFTERTHOUGHT:

Magazine editors do something that makes writers furious. When they return an article or story with a rejection slip, or even a nice little note, they fasten the slip or note to the manuscript with a paper clip. The result is that the neatly typed pages, otherwise in pristine condition, bear the mark of the clip—a clear indication that the manuscript has been submitted somewhere and returned.

What does the writer do before he tries another magazine? He can retype the whole manuscript. He can retype the first page and hope the next editor doesn't notice that the type on the first page is a little lighter and there is a paper clip mark on each of the succeeding pages. He can write an unnecessary little note, perhaps saying "I hope you like the enclosed," and affix it with a paper clip, making sure the clip fits into the original clip marks.

Or he can iron out the marks. This is a method I tried once. A friend of mine, always ready with advice, suggested it to me. I set up the ironing board, got the electric iron good and hot, and worked on those clip marks as if I were ironing out the wrinkles in a pair of pants. But the marks stubbornly remained. The editor had apparently used Permanent Press paper clips.

If I ever come face-to-face with an editor who puts paper clips on manuscripts he returns, I swear I'll put a large-size paper clip on his nose. And maybe one on each ear. I hope they leave unremovable marks.

Yes, Virginia, There Is a Thanksgiving

You probably think the first Thanksgiving was celebrated by the Massachusetts Pilgrims in 1621, after the first good harvest. If that is what you think, you are wrong.

Historians now agree, if they agree on anything, that the first Thanksgiving took place in Virginia on December 4, 1619, almost two years before the event in Massachusetts.

In 1962 the Honorary Chairman of the Richmond Thanksgiving Festival wired President Kennedy, protesting the erroneous credit given to Massachusetts in the President's Thanksgiving Proclamation. Historian Arthur Schlesinger, Jr., apologized on the President's behalf. "You are quite right," he said, "and I can only plead an unconquerable New England bias on the part of the White House staff. I can assure you that the error will not be repeated."

In his next proclamation, President Kennedy made everyone happy by declaring: "Over three centuries ago, our forefathers in Virginia and in Massachusetts, far from home in a lonely wilderness, set aside a time of Thanksgiving." He did not give up completely on his home state, but at least he named Virginia first.

Anyhow, if you have been picturing the first Thanksgiving as one when dour Pilgrims sat around and ate turkey, you had better revise the picture. Imagine, instead, not-so-dour Virginians sitting around eating baked ham.

But don't be too quick to praise the Virginians for giving thanks two years before the Pilgrims. After all, the Pilgrims arrived in 1620 and gave thanks in 1621, waiting only a year. The Virginians, on the other hand, arrived in 1607 and didn't give thanks for twelve years. Either they were a long time getting a good harvest or they wanted to be sure before they committed themselves.

It may be only a coincidence, but in 1619, the year of their first Thanksgiving, the Virginia colonists received an unusual shipment from England—a boatload of young women. Lonely young settlers had ordered them from a mail-order (or female-order) catalogue.

They cost 120 pounds of tobacco each, and many a young man had to choose between smoking and marrying. Fortunately, Rudyard Kipling had not yet written his touching line: "And a woman is only a woman, but a good cigar is a smoke." Otherwise the young men might have held onto their tobacco.

So it was that the first Thanksgiving in Massachusetts gave thanks for a fine crop of corn, while the first Thanksgiving in Virginia may have given thanks for a bountiful bevy of women. If so, it was the last public celebration offering thanks for women until the establishment of Mother's Day in 1914.

During the Revolutionary War, Americans were more thankful than they ever have been since. Eight special days of thanks were observed when victories were won. When there was a defeat, people just sat around in silence or blamed the administration.

For a while Thanksgiving Day was left up to the states. Some states had it and some didn't, as is true today of daylight-saving time. It was hard on the makers of greeting cards. Imagine getting a fancy card, saying, "Happy Thanksgiving. Don't eat too much turkey," when it wasn't Thanksgiving in your state, and you were having ground round for dinner.

In 1830 New York became the first state to have an official Thanksgiving Day. Those who think the people of New York had more to be thankful for than the people of, say, Pennsylvania, are mistaken. More likely, many people were getting ready to move out of New York, and it was thought they might be persuaded to stay if they were promised an extra holiday.

In 1863, busy as he was with the Civil War, Abraham Lincoln issued a Thanksgiving Day proclamation setting aside the fourth Thursday of November as "a day of thanksgiving and praise to our beneficent Father." Coming from Honest Abe, this had a lot of impact on people. If President Lincoln could give thanks, with all the trouble he had on his hands, they guessed they could, too.

When Lincoln did the same thing again in 1864, two years in a row, it became a tradition. Thanksgiving was celebrated each year on the fourth Thursday in November by Republicans and Democrats alike.

Then in 1939 President Franklin D. Roosevelt took one of his most drastic actions. He decreed that Thanksgiving Day would be celebrated one week earlier! His motives, he said, were humanitarian: he wished to give people time to eat up the last of their Thanksgiving turkey before starting on their Christmas turkey. But this led to a clash between the turkey growers and the bicarbonate-of-soda makers and gave the Republicans a campaign issue.

Finally Congress ruled that after 1941 the fourth Thursday of November would be observed as Thanksgiving and would be a legal holiday. Any other day would be an illegal holiday. The United States was about to enter World War II, and Congress wanted to impress the enemy with a show of national unity.

Each year, as we celebrate Thanksgiving Day, let us remember how it was among our forefathers in Massachusetts. Or, even earlier, in Virginia. Or, earlier still, before the arrival of either the Pilgrims or the Virginians.

"Let us be thankful," an Indian chief might have proclaimed to his followers back in 1606, "that we still have the place to ourselves."

AFTERTHOUGHT:

Whatever the place and date of the original Thanksgiving, all too many of us, I fear, bow our heads only to get our mouths closer to the plate. Consider the following postprandial lines:

> When Thanksgiving dinner is over, I know
> Just what I shall do and just where I shall go:
> As soon as I've finished and feel that I'm able,
> I'll hoist myself up from my place at the table,
> Take six or eight steps standing upright, though curved,
> And plunk myself down in a spot I've reserved.
> The rest of the day, folks, that's me over there—
> The overstuffed chap in the overstuffed chair.

Yes, I know it should be "that's I" in the next-to-last line. But I am mindful of the purist who was careful always to say "It is I." One day he fell into an abandoned well and for hours screamed for help. Rescuers, hearing his shouts, arrived at last and peered over the edge into the blackness.

"Who's down there?" one of them asked.

"It's me!" "It's me!" screamed the purist.

Had he said, "It is I," I am not sure they would have pulled him up.

But getting back to the original Thanksgiving. Whether it was in Virgina or Massachusetts, I am sure there were celebrants who overate or ate something that disagreed with them. Those who got really sick didn't realize how lucky they were to have the woods all around them. Compare this with having to go to the bathroom and finding somebody already in there.

Long Distance Doesn't
Lend Enchantment

One thing often happens when I make a long-distance call. Just about the time I have had my say and am thinking of winding up, something goes wrong and I am cut off. I say something goes wrong, but for all I know the telephone company keeps someone on duty just for this purpose.

"Hello," I say. "Hello, hello." I have a feeling that if one "Hello" gets no response, two or three will. "Hello, hello," I repeat, for good measure.

For a while there is a dead silence, or perhaps a buzzing sound. Between the two, I prefer a buzzing sound, because this indicates that the power is on, even if it isn't transmitting my voice. Then I click the receiver a few times. I am not sure whether anyone else hears the clicking, but I do, and for a moment think I have broken an eardrum.

86

Finally the operator comes on.

"May I help you?" she asks.

"I've been cut off," I say.

"What number were you calling?" she asks. "Do you want me to place your call again?"

"No, I guess not," I say. "I was just about through anyhow."

So I put up the phone and go about my business. Or I try to, but I begin to think that the party I was calling will think that I had hung up on him and was mad about something.

After a moment of indecision, I dial the operator.

"I would like to place that call again," I tell her, giving her all the necessary information once more.

"The line is busy," she says after a bit. I can hear the busy signal.

"He is probably trying to get me," I say. "He thinks I think he hung up on me."

That, of course, is precisely what has happened.

With my trying to get through to him and his trying to get through to me, each of us is becoming more and more concerned about what the other must think about being hung up on. We are at a stalemate, like two people trying to pass each other in a narrow doorway, and making their moves at the same time.

Finally, thanks to the law of averages or something, he gets through to me or I get through to him.

"We must have been cut off," I say.

"Yes, we must have been cut off," he says.

He is relieved that now I know he didn't hang up on me, and I am relieved that now he knows I didn't hang up on him. For a moment there is silence, both of us feeling pretty good about the whole thing.

"I really didn't have anything more to say," I tell him.

"I didn't have anything more to say either," he says.

"I was just about to say good-bye," I say.
"I was just about to say good-bye, too," he says.
"Well, good-bye," I say.
"Good-bye," he says.

AFTERTHOUGHT:

Everyone knows that Alexander Graham Bell invented the telephone. But not everyone is aware that but for a decision of the United States Supreme Court, credit for this important invention would have gone to Elisha Gray. Bell was granted a patent for the telephone in 1876, but only after the Supreme Court decided that he had beaten out Gray by a hair, or perhaps we should say a wire. Descendants of Elisha Gray know what a difference it makes to come in second.

But for Alexander Graham Bell (and Elisha Gray) we might not today have the party line, the wrong number, and the busy signal.

Bell invented not only the telephone but the graphophone, a forerunner of the phonograph. If he had just got the name turned around right, he might have made it ahead of Thomas A. Edison. At least now he knew how Elisha Gray felt.

Bell lived for almost fifty years after inventing the telephone. Always experimenting, he tossed cats out of a window to try to figure out why they always landed on their feet. "He'll always land on his feet," people said of Alex, who was a resourceful fellow, but no one ever threw him out of a window to verify this statement.

What Bell failed to develop was a telephone that would not always stop ringing just one ring before you get to it.

Confessions of a
Cold-Cure Collector

For several years I have been collecting cures for the common cold. They are much easier to accumulate than stamps, rare coins, autographs of film stars, or matchbooks. People who have unusual cures for the common cold are very generous with them. I have never had to pay a penny.

However there are difficulties. Unlike the collector of stamps and rare coins, the collector of cold cures is unable to shop around in cold-cure stores. Nor can he subscribe to a magazine, such as *The Cold-Cure Collector,* and read articles on the subject and examine the ads for "Cures Wanted," "Cures for Sale," and "Will Exchange." It is a very individual enterprise and has to be done on a person-to-person basis.

I have picked up cures, as well as colds, from my next-door neighbor, a helpful fellow who leans over the fence and coughs into my face. I have learned about cures at the office, at parties, on the golf course, going up (or down) in an elevator, on trains and planes, and sitting on a bar stool. This last is one of the most productive, since I get cures not only from the persons on the stools to my left and right but from the bartender—who has heard everything.

Out of the hundreds of cures I have garnered, in a collection I am bequeathing to the American Medical Association, I shall mention only a few. If I have overlooked your favorite cure, please do not write me. It is probably in my file under A ("Asafetida") or Z ("Zodiac Signs and Sinuses").

One cure that intrigues me, but that I have never tried, is to stand on your head. I don't mean for me to stand on your head (which is a cure I just now thought of), but for you, the cold sufferer, to upend yourself. The theory behind this, as it was explained to me, is that the blood comes rushing down from the rest of the body and goes to work on the cold, which is lodged in the membranes of the nose and throat. The reason I have never tried this cure is that I am unable to stand on my head without getting a crick in my neck, and a crick in my neck hurts a lot worse than a cold in my nose or chest.

But if blood is good for a cold, why not just drink a glass of Type O, or whatever is your favorite, with meals and at bedtime? Surprisingly, no one has suggested this to me. Many physicians, it is true, say, "Drink plenty of liquids," and since they rarely say which liquids, blood may be the sort of thing they have in mind. Anyhow, I wish I knew whether vampires ever catch cold. If they don't, I see a great scientific breakthrough here and a chance to make millions.

During the height of the chlorophyll craze, back in the mid-fifties, when everything from chewing gum to laxative tablets was green, I heard about a fascinating cure for a cold. It was to chew clover, freshly plucked. Nothing was said about the special potency of an occasional four-leaf clover, the stress being on freshness and on chewing the clover thoroughly before swallowing it. All that chlorophyll was sure to do something for you.

I tried it, and it did something for me. It stained my teeth a bright green. That was all right on St. Patrick's Day, but the rest of the time I went around trying to keep my mouth shut, which many thought an improvement. I couldn't see that it did anything for my cold, but it had a beneficial side, or rather front, effect. You see, our neighbors have dichondra (which is not a disease but a ground cover), while our front lawn has clover. When I told them about this cold cure, they came over and clawed away until they thought they had enough for a full treatment. For almost three weeks I didn't have to mow.

Another interesting cure is to hold your breath. If holding your breath will stop hiccups, why won't it stop a cold? After all, hiccups also have to do with the respiratory system and are a form of cough (hiccough). Holding your breath strengthens your lungs, and anyone whose cold has gone into pneumonia knows how important it is to have strong lungs. But I have never found out how long one should hold one's breath. If holding my breath has never cured a cold for me, it may be because I have not held my breath quite long enough. Another thirty seconds might have done the trick. But I tend to black out. I am sure that if I could stop breathing long enough —say an hour—I would get over my cold. In fact I would never have one again.

My wife's favorite cold cure is to snuff up salt water. She does this by putting some salt in a glass of water, then pouring the salted water into her cupped hand and snuffing the stuff up her nose. This produces a set of noises that, if you heard them once, you would always remember. If you want to know what a hippopotamus sounds like, wallowing around in a muddy stream, you can save yourself a trip to darkest Africa.

Speaking of travel, it is my wife's contention that snuffing up a salt solution in our bathroom is no substitute for snuffing up sea water at an expensive seaside resort. The salt water of the sea is Nature's mixture, exactly as salty as it should be. And the salt is different too, perhaps enriched by chemicals from kelp and dead fish.

Anyhow, whenever my wife gets a cold she insists that we take off for Bermuda, Florida, or Hawaii, so she can snuff properly salted sea water. I ask only that she get out far enough so that people on the beach can't see, or hear, what she's doing. The cure might catch on, and I can't bear to think of swimming where hundreds of people, standing in the shallow water, are busy snuffing.

One trouble with cold cures is that one cure sometimes cancels out another. Thus, many physicians recommend going to bed and resting when you have a cold. But you may also have been advised to get outdoors and exercise. This makes you breathe deeply, strengthens the heart, and starts the blood coursing into places where it's needed. I'm a middle-of-the-roader and don't wish to hurt anyone's feelings, so I do both. I go out and exercise and then I go to bed and rest a while, then I go out and exercise and then I go to bed and rest a while. I am not sure whether this helps my cold any, but it has the virtue of keeping me busy.

In fact, I suppose the best advice about a cold, though it's hardly a cure, is to keep so busy doing something that you forget you have a cold. For instance, you can occupy yourself as I do, collecting cold cures. If enough people become interested, I'm going to invite them to join me in a group called the American Collectors of Homemade Otolaryngological Oddities—or ACHOO.

Just one other thing. You often hear someone say, "I've got a bad cold." Did you ever hear anyone say, "I've got a good cold?"

Maybe the common cold is just getting back at us for being so uncomplimentary.

AFTERTHOUGHT:

I suppose a cold is called a cold not because one is cold, since a cold accompanied by a fever makes one hot, but because "cold" is a four-letter word with rather unpleasant connotations. Consider what it is to have cold feet or to be considered cold-hearted or to be given the cold shoulder or to break out in a cold sweat or to be murdered in cold blood, perhaps with a cold chisel. A cold sore, as a matter of fact, is not caused by a cold but by a fever that may arise from almost any ailment. It is probably called a cold sore simply because it is so ugly and bothersome.

Most of my friends, I notice, seldom say they have a cold. They say they have a bug. Or they say they have a virus. If they have a head cold and are making a bid for attention and sympathy they may even say, "I have a bad case of coryza." Coryza sounds better, somehow, than nasal catarrh.

Medical scientists may someday find a cure for the common cold. I mean a cure that works. If they do, and if they also learn how to control the weather, what will there be left to talk about?

Incident in Japan

I have often wondered what it would be like to be among strangers, of both sexes, with no clothes on. Would I be embarrassed, self-conscious, ill-at-ease? Or would I be completely poised and debonair, a nude Man of Distinction?

To find out, I have long thought of joining a nudist colony, but so far have been unable to discover such a group in or near my place of residence, a college town dominated by retired missionaries. Also, I have usually had such thoughts along about midwinter, when the idea of a nude romp in the woods left me cold.

It began to look as if I would never know how I would react to being nude in public any more than, having been a desk soldier in World War II, I would know whether I would be brave or cowardly under fire. It was my lot, apparently, to go through life untested.

Then I had occasion to go to Japan, and at once realized that the opportunity of which I had dreamed was within my grasp. A few months earlier, while examining a book on Japanese culture, I had found, amongst the photographs of gardens and temples, a photo under which was written: "The Japanese are scrupulously clean. Picture of public bath in Kyoto." My interest in Japanese temples and gardens, which had never been strong, now disappeared entirely. In its place came thoughts, not all of them scrupulously clean, of public baths, and I had a new and compelling reason for going to Japan.

Not to appear too eager, I did not at once hunt up a public bath when I arrived in the land of the rising sun. Guidebook in hand, I joined a party of tourists and visited a few temples first. But my thoughts, I fear, were not upon the delicate curve of the gray tile roofs, or on the symbolism of the rock gardens, or on the guide's statement, dutifully recorded by my fellow tourists, that "This famous statue of Buddha, which weighs 452 tons, is 53.5 feet in height and has thumbs 4.8 feet long." My mind was filled with visions of myself consorting in a bath with delicately curved Japanese, and to heck with the length of their thumbs. My palms perspired freely, thanks to anticipation mingled with fear, though the winter afternoon was cold enough for overcoats and mufflers.

My own notebook carried only one page of notes, jotted down after studiously careful inquiry of the guide while traveling between the fifth temple and the sixth. These were instructions concerning the name and address of a public bath in Kyoto.

"Have you ever been there yourself?" I asked.

"No," said the guide, without amplification. From his expression of distaste I gathered that, however it may have been in old Japan, the public bath is now considered a little low class, and is chiefly frequented, especially in rural districts, by persons whose homes are without the requisite plumbing. I refer now to the genuine public bath, low priced and used for getting clean (as well as relaxing and socializing with the neighbors), and not the gaudier version, or "recreation bath," which is for the tired businessman in no hurry to get home.

That night, girding my loins (which were so soon to be ungirded), I sought out the bathhouse—down a maze of narrow streets with an occasional dimly glowing Japanese lantern, and past tiny restaurants specializing in raw fish, where no more than five or six persons at a time could wield their chopsticks. People coming out of these restaurants glanced curiously at this incongruous American, far from the tourist hotels frequented by his kind.

At last I reached the place, recognizing the Japanese symbol for bath or, more accurately, "place of hot water," which had been described for me. After a moment's hesitation I went into the foyer, where men and women were paying the 100-yen entrance fee (about 28 cents) and leaving their shoes with an attendant who, like a hat-check girl or car parker, took them away and placed them on a shelf. Slippers were supplied in their stead.

At this point I observed, with a combination of disappointment and relief, that the women proceeded toward a bathroom on this main floor, while the men descended the stairs to the floor below. Making a quick decision, since I doubt that any choice was open to me, I followed the men. No one understanding a word of English, it seemed futile to ask for the manager and complain that this was not precisely according to the photo in the book on Japanese culture.

The Japanese, undistracted by such thoughts and better able to keep their slippers on, moved briskly down the stairs and through swinging doors, while this lone and somewhat jittery Caucasian shuffled along. Beyond the swinging doors we came into a room lined on two sides by wooden lockers. On a third side were three low-backed chairs and a counter behind which stood a middle-aged woman cashier. Clustered around her were four or five attractive Japanese girls, ages maybe sixteen to eighteen, busily chattering to one another. On the four sides were glass doors beyond which I could see the bath, a slight mist of steam giving it a romantic, exotic look.

As I could tell from the actions of my bathmates, the time had come for me to disrobe. Turning my back to the girls, a few feet away at the counter (a modesty not affected by the Japanese on either side of me), I stripped, putting my clothes in a wicker basket which I then placed in a locker. Emulating the others, I slipped over my wrist the elastic bracelet to which the locker key was attached. As I stood there, slightly crouched, fashioning a kind of fig leaf out of my clasped hands, I felt a tap on my shoulder.

"*Dozo,*" came a pleasant female voice. As I half turned, a towel smaller than a pocket handkerchief was thrust toward me.

"*Arigato gozaimasu,*" I said, grabbing the snippet of cloth with one hand I could ill spare, and in a reckless burst using up two of my ten words of Japanese.

Girding my loins again, this time with a loin cloth which would go neither between nor around and therefore had to be held in place, I followed a couple of Japanese gentlemen, at a discreet distance from their bare backsides, through the doors and into the bathing room. One wore his towel as I did, but the other, probably a regular customer, nonchalantly held it at his side as he strode past the cashier and the girl attendants.

"*Banzai,*" I muttered faintly, dipping my towel ever so slightly in the salute of one passing in review.

In the bathroom probably twenty men sat on low wooden stools along a row of hot and cold water faucets a foot or so off the floor. Each had taken a small basin from a pile, and after filling this and soaping his tiny towel (now become washrag), busily got to work lathering himself all over. Some shaved with small razors, bought at a counter, which were discarded after one use.

As I watched the procedure, imitatively soaping and rinsing myself, two of the young women I had seen by the counter, one in white shorts and a snug blue sweater and the other, doubtless warmer-blooded, in bra and shorts, circulated among the men, recovering a cake of soap that had slipped away or picking up stools and basins no longer in use and returning them to the pile.

By now not only soaped and rinsed but fairly well adjusted, I sauntered to the large bath in the center of the room, a circular pool perhaps three or four feet deep, in which a dozen or so men were soaking. No one paid the slightest attention to me, and since I could think of nothing but *Ohayo gozaimasu,* "Good morning," and it was then after 8:00 P.M., I was unable to get up a conversation. After a few minutes of soaking and meditating, I remembered another bit of Japanese, *Benjo wa doko desu ka,* "Where is the toilet?" but this also seemed a poor opening gambit.

Becoming faint from unaccustomed immersion in almost boiling water, I finally crawled out and went back by the faucets to fill my basin with a little cold water and throw it over me before I passed out. At this point I noticed the two girls, the one in the blue sweater and the one in the bra, bustling around the room and calling out as if they were vending something, though they seemed to have nothing for sale. Since, from time to time, they stopped behind one of the bathers and began scrubbing him, I suspect their cry was the Japanese equivalent of "Wancher back scrubbed?" My back itched with pleasurable anticipation.

Sitting on my little wooden stool, I waited until the girl in the blue sweater was free. For some reason, perhaps the color of her sweater, I preferred her to the one in the bra. Catching her eye, I waved as if beckoning a waiter or calling a taxi, and she came running. In a moment she was in position. A few seconds later I felt her sudsy hand on my back. Ah. . . .

But this gentle caress was not to last. Once I was thoroughly soaped, from neck to hips, I began to feel the heavy-handed scrape of what I imagined was a steel file or a coarse floor brush. Later I was told it was a dried gourd with inch-long spikes. As this instrument raked my back under the full pressure of my sweater girl, whose arm muscles I had not previously noticed, I tried to keep from flinching and from making grimaces of pain. Harder and harder she rubbed, down through the epidermis, dermis, and, I felt sure, through muscle tissue into my spine and rib cage.

Concerned as I was about the possibility of permanent injury, and trying to get up courage to see whether what was trickling from my back was soapy water or blood, I forgot to hold my washrag in its proper place. Even as she continued to scrub with one hand, my girl reached down with the other hand and retrieved it.

"*Dozo,*" she said, handing it to me.

"*Arigato gozaimasu,*" I murmured, restoring the postage stamp to the male.

While she scraped away, she kept up a constant conversation with her colleague in the bra, who was working on the back of a gentleman in front of me. From time to time she would say something and laugh loudly, and the bra girl would dart a look in my direction and join in the laughter. Whatever they were talking about they were obviously laughing at, not admiring. I held my washcloth firmly in place with both hands, stretching it as much as possible, and tried not to reveal how deeply I was hurt— my ego as well as my back.

Finally, with a few last rubs, calculated, I think, to

work salt into my wounds, sweater girl poured several basins of scalding water over me, sloshing me in the front as well as the rear. But for alertness on my part, my cloth would have washed off and gone down the drain. Could she have had this in mind? She and her pal were, by this time, looking at me brazenly, even pointing, and laughing almost hysterically. Suddenly my girl grabbed my left arm and lifted it up. I wondered—did she want to dance, perhaps hoping I would teach her the latest American step?

But no, she thrust a second elastic bracelet over my outstretched arm, a bracelet like the one with my locker key except that this bore a bright red tag of plastic, with "100" on it. Could it mean that I was now 100 percent clean? With my two arm pieces dangling, I felt like posing for a painting entitled Nude Wearing a Charm Bracelet.

Still wet, and unable to dry myself with my sopping piece of cloth, I left the bathroom and went into the locker room, planning to dress and get the hell out of there. But now I saw the use of the three chairs by the cash register. Two of them were occupied by naked Japanese gentlemen having a massage while they sat there stolidly, their wet little towels rather rakishly draped over whatever they considered private in a public bath.

I climbed into the third chair and made motions at my back, trying to indicate the need for some Mercurochrome and bandages. But a girl in a black sweater (or mostly in it), thinking I wanted a massage, began to dig her thumbs into my neck and beat my back with her fists as though she hated me for something I had done or failed to do to her. Now and then she punctuated her efforts by leaning into me with her elbows. An occasional hard blow, lower down, was I am sure with her feet.

When she finished, with two or three left hooks that

had me reeling, she seized my arm from behind, drew it sharply back and up in a judo hold, and slipped a third elastic bracelet over my wrist, this one bearing a yellow tag. In view of the courage (along with no telling what else) I had displayed, the color could have had no relationship to my character.

"*Arigato gozaimasu,*" I said, though I felt no thanks were due.

"*Dozo,*" she replied, and managed to keep a straight face for a moment before going into a convulsion. She laughed even harder as I struggled up from my stool, turned my scarred backside to her, and staggered toward my locker. By this time I had given up trying to hold my cloth in position, possessing neither the modesty nor the strength.

My shirt went on a little hard, over the open wounds, but at last I was dressed. At the cash register I surrendered my red and yellow tags and found that my back scrub and my massage had cost 100 yen each. With the original 100 yen for the bath, I had paid a total of 300 yen (84 cents) for an evening of good clean fun, Japanese style. Up the stairs I went, and out to the foyer.

"*Sayonara,*" I said, after recovering my shoes from the doorman and exchanging deep bows, mine achieved somewhat painfully.

I walked back up the narrow streets, under Japanese lanterns, and past the raw-fish restaurants. Four things were clear to me: (1) I was clean, (2) I had lost a large area of valuable skin, (3) I was capable of walking around naked in public with almost no embarrassment, and (4) seen in the nude, I was uninteresting to men and ridiculous to young women, who found me hilarious.

Now, or as soon as I was able to walk without pain when my shirt scraped my back, I could look at the temples and gardens with the other tourists—nice people who, having seen me only with my clothes on, took me seriously.

AFTERTHOUGHT:

Only recently I learned that some of the public baths in Japan are equipped with peepholes. For a few hundred yen, maybe a dollar or so, anyone who would rather peek than participate can stand outside the bathing room and get an eyeful. This raises a few personal questions. Was my bath in Kyoto so equipped? If so, how big a crowd did I draw? And finally, am I entitled to a percentage of the gate?

All I know is that if I have any yen coming to me, I'm not going back to collect. Chances are, the peephole customers demanded their money back anyhow.

The Other Side of
the Coin

Teenagers think their parents are made of money, and that all they—the teenagers—have to do when they want some is to break off a little piece. What they don't know is how much it hurts.

Some exceptional teenagers don't think like this. They think their parents are more like a bank—a bank that permits unlimited withdrawals without demanding an occasional deposit. At this wild bank, teenagers don't have to write a check; they just go up to the teller and tell him how much they want. (They tell the teller, you will notice; the teller doesn't tell them.) However much they may want, there is always more back there in the parent-vault.

At least there had better be. It does no good for a parent to plead poverty. If a parent says, "It's taking every cent I earn to pay the rent and food bills," the teenager will come back with helpful suggestions for ways the parent can increase the family income: night work, or asking the boss for a raise, or cutting out golf, or some similar deprivation. Or the teenager will say, "What did you have children for, if you can't support them?"

Sometimes a parent makes a mistake, such as asking, "Why don't you go out and earn the money for yourself? You could mow lawns or wash cars or something." The reason this is a mistake is that it triggers a carefully rehearsed, righteously indignant response, delivered with one hand pressed against the forehead and with eyes closed in an expression of great pain.

"If I get a job, I'll be taking work away from somebody who has a wife and children to support," the teenager says. Or, "I must save my time for homework. You want me to get good grades, don't you?" (The parent does, no doubt about that, considering the latest report card.) Or, "Youth is a time to be savored. You've said that yourself." (It *is* an exact quote, but taken from a speech on the ills of going steady.) Then comes the clincher: "I'll have the rest of my life to work."

Teenagers don't really want money; they want what it buys. Money itself only collects interest. The interest on a dollar is only about five cents a year—and what can you buy for five cents nowadays?

To teenagers, money is strictly for spending. They can't bear to have the stuff just lying around. They keep their cash in their hands, ready to spend at the first opportunity.

And there are plenty of opportunities. What teenagers can't get in a store, they can order by mail. All those books lying around? They aren't required reading for English or history. Those are mail-order catalogues. In comes a catalogue, out goes an envelope full of cash. The stamps on the envelope (and an envelope full of dimes and quarters can be mighty heavy) were supplied by the parent, who keeps stamps on his desk (next to the envelopes).

Once a teenager makes a purchase, that's only the beginning. Let's say it's a surfboard. A surfboard requires all sorts of upkeep, such as gold leaf for the owner's name and his coat of arms. A record player takes records. A guitar takes strings. A radio takes batteries, and batteries, and batteries.

One thing about a teenager's purchase—it's always a necessity. In fact it's a matter of life or death. There is no such thing as a luxury. When a teenager asks a parent for money to buy something he just can't live without—say an imported ivory ball to replace the standard knob on his car's gearshift lever—he has tears in his eyes and a catch in his voice. He is pleading desperately for his very existence, socially. He is a pitiful sight. Fortunately, he snaps back to normal (loud and cocky) as soon as he gets what he wants.

Parents have no defense against a teenager who *has* to have money. If Dad doesn't have it, he can always borrow it.

He might, cheerfully, put up his teenager as collateral.

AFTERTHOUGHT:

I thought of calling this, to paraphrase Tom Paine, "These Are the Teens that Try Men's Souls." It is one of many pieces I wrote for *American Youth,* a magazine given by General Motors to every teenager in the United States on gaining a driver's license. My articles were calculated to annoy these young readers into writing a response that would demolish my arguments.

The editors gave a prize of one hundred dollars to the author of the best essay, and the combination of my insolence and the cash invariably brought thousands of rejoinders. I have read many of these and am forced to admit, however reluctantly, that some of them put me down very effectively.

Going to the Dog

Walking the dog is a favorite means of exercise, especially for city dwellers. The only unfortunate thing about this is that the dog, a sleek, lean creature, gets most of the exercise. While his flabby master walks slowly down the sidewalk, the trim, superbly muscled dog runs from side to side and in circles, covering at least half a mile for every block traversed by his human companion.

It would be much better if the two could reverse their roles, the dog taking the direct route and his master darting to-and-fro, burning up fat and reducing the cholesterol in his bloodstream. Such a switch would, however, be hard to manage, even though the dog's owner might enjoy, just for once, running around and around his dog, and getting him completely tangled up in the leash.

Since it would be difficult for the dog and his master to change places, the dog finding it clumsy to hold the end of the leash with his paw, I have another suggestion. What I propose is for the dog's master to let the leash go slack and move with the dog. This would entail (a word that seems peculiarly apt) stopping suddenly to sniff something or other, and then taking off like a sprinter leaving his starting block. It would mean chasing another dog or cat at full speed, and hoping the other dog or cat didn't stand and fight. This stopping and starting, these bursts of speed, would be just the thing for developing the leg and thigh muscles and for helping the lungs and the heart.

Outside the city, in rural areas where there is no leash law, or it is not observed, the owner of a dog could really get himself in shape by sticking close to the dog as it ran across fields, doubled back and forth while following a scent, and jumped at tree trunks in an attempt to get at a squirrel on an upper branch. It would be a great game of follow-the-leader. The man's pulse would beat fast, his breathing would be deep, and the proponents of aerobics would heartily approve.

As for the dog, think of how he would enjoy his master's side-by-side participation, whether bounding across a field, looking down a gopher hole, or savoring a fireplug. As anyone knows, it's not much fun doing things alone. Many a time the dog must have longed for someone to share his adventures and discoveries. How wistfully he looked back at his master, plodding along on the sidewalk or path, missing so much and being so much missed. . . .

One thing I know. He who, instead of walking his dog, runs with him and ventures with him, will sleep well at night. Unless, that is, he is awakened by the mournful howl of some dog who has seen the man and dog together and wishes *his* master, too, would be that kind of companion.

Try it sometime—not walking the dog but dogging the walk. It might be advisable, however, to go to your physician for a checkup first.

AFTERTHOUGHT:

We always had a dog until my wife ran over Happy, some years ago. She didn't mean to do it. She just backed the car out without looking, and Happy was in the way. Fortunately I was at the office and didn't see this tragic episode. If it had to happen, it was better for my wife to feel the bump and hear the mournful howl and pick up the poor creature, its back broken, and look into its big brown eyes, full of sadness and pain, and take it to the vet to be put out of its misery. My wife is a woman of strong character, not given to emotion. She can stand either actual or vicarious suffering far better than I.

We never got another dog. I prefer just to remember Happy. But I can never get away completely from dogs or the dog concept. I write what some people call doggerel. These same people think me dogmatic. My books are dog-eared. I am often in the doghouse. I sometimes put on the dog. I once made a birdie on a five-par dogleg hole. And there is no question that I am gradually going to the dogs.

Especially since my wife ran over Happy.

Their Breath Is Sweet,
Their Skin Is Pure

The other day I came upon something in the newspaper that startled me. It was not an airplane crash or a murder or a military coup. Such things no longer startle me—in fact they seem hardly news.

What I read about had social and perhaps political significance. Its impact on the Gross National Product and all that sort of thing was simply (or complexly) enormous.

Not to keep you in suspense any longer, the item I ran across was as follows: "Men are now spending more than one billion dollars a year for grooming products and services, including manicures." Think of it! Or, if you want to give your will power a real workout, try not to think of it. As happens when anything shakes my central nervous system, it compelled me to express myself in verse:

> One thing today that's clearly booming,
> Besides artillery, is grooming.
> Now men are smooth on cheek and chin,

Their hair is neat, however thin,
Their teeth are brushed four times a day
With dentifrice that routs decay,
Their breath is sweet, their skin is pure,
From morn to night they're always sure.
We would not for the world suggest
It's wrong for men to look their best
And as they come into a room
Waft scents of masculine perfume.
We only say that we foresee
A time when bathrooms will not be
Quite big enough for bottles, cans,
And sundry tubes and boxes. Plans
Must henceforth face the facts of life:
A man needs shelves more than his wife,
Indeed, with things that spray and foam,
Should have a drugstore in his home.

What really fascinates me, you see, is not the economic consequences of expenditure of one billion dollars a year by men who are trying to look better and smell better. It is the impact on that most important room in the house, the bathroom. Since no man, or woman, can throw away a box with one pill in it, even though what the pill is good for has long since been forgotten, or discard a bottle with a half inch of stuff in the bottom, and since containers (in the Large Economy Size) are getting larger and larger and in ever fancier shapes—I honestly don't see where we are going to put it all.

It was bad enough when a wife took up the three top shelves in the medicine chest and left the bottom one for her husband. It got worse when her hormone cold cream and depilatory and eye shadow and deodorant and bath crystals and after-bath oils and dusting powders began to cover all available space from the bathtub to the wash basin. This, of course, was back when a man was content with a toothbrush, toothpaste, shaving cream, a razor, a comb, a hairbrush, and, if he was a bit of a dude, some after-shave lotion that had a lot of smell for the price.

But those were the Good Old Days, when a man thought his skin was meant only to keep his insides in, and it was not necessary that it be smooth and beautiful and scented with some odor of the spicy or leathery sort attractive to women. Today, if he is to make his little contribution to that billion-a-year industry, his shaving cream must whoosh out of a pressurized can, his skin must be lubricated by an oil with a secret ingredient developed by the National Space Agency and endorsed by four out of five astronauts, and his hair must be treated regularly with a tonic that not only leaves no trace of oil when a beautiful lady runs her white-gloved hand over his head but makes it possible to wear a navy blue suit without having to carry a whiskbroom.

Where are men to keep their billion-dollar loot, added to no telling how many billion dollars' worth lugged home by women? My suggestion is that architects start right now to design the Home of Tomorrow, with one bedroom, a two-car garage, and three bathrooms, for the couple who have everything—everything, that is, in the way of cosmetics. One bathroom would be for the husband, one for the wife, and one for the storage of spare tweezers and the like. This should suffice, if there are plenty of built-in cabinets, until the children come along. Then the formula should be: for every 12 x 12 bedroom a 20 x 20 bathroom. Especially for teenagers, who spend more of their time in the bathroom than in the bedroom anyhow. . . .

For a moment, preoccupied by that billion-dollar outlay by men for grooming, I forgot the words "including manicures." I have no ideas about how to get men to cut down on the purchase of skin lotions and hair tonics, with their inevitable effect on medicine chests and bathrooms if not on skin and hair. But if you want to reduce and perhaps eliminate manicures, in order to divert the money to national defense, foreign aid, or the elimination of poverty, I have the answer.

Male manicurists.

AFTERTHOUGHT:

My own medicine chest is crowded more with pills, ointments, cough syrups, vitamins, and the like than with grooming products. I am more concerned with staying alive than with being beautiful. As a matter of fact medical science has come to my rescue repeatedly, curing me of all manner of ailments, while I have had little help from cosmetology. I know what to use for a cough or for athlete's foot, but I have yet to find a preparation that will keep my hair from thinning, my jowls from thickening, my liver spots from spreading, my wrinkles from deepening, and the bags under my eyes from growing baggier.

It is the mirror on my medicine chest that troubles me more than finding room for some new pharmaceutical item inside it. If I could learn to shave without looking at myself in the mirror, I would be a much happier man. That first glimpse I have of myself in the morning, before I have shaved and before my eyes have cleared, gives me a depressing start for the day. I might have said merely that it gives me a start, though I am beginning to know what to expect. There is only one compensation. A flaw in the mirror has a way of spreading my nose across my face and making me look truly hideous. When I move a little, to avoid this effect, and discover that I am really not repulsive, only homely, I am grateful. Things could be worse, I think, and I emerge from the bathroom with enough courage to face the world with my face.

A Short History of
the Embrace

The embrace probably began in the Stone Age,
when some Stone Age man who had been lifting
stones suddenly took it into his head to lift a woman.
It is not known why he decided to do this, deviating from
current practice and running the risk of being called a
deviationist.

One theory, advanced by some scholars, is that the
woman was standing on a stone the man wished to lift.
Another is that she was sitting on it. Still another is that
she was lying on it, with an inscrutable look in her eyes.

Scholars disagree even more violently about why the
Stone Age man was so intent on lifting this particular
stone, with so many others lying around. Perhaps there
was something underneath it, such as another woman,
whom he had pinned down with the stone to be sure she
would be there when he came back. Or maybe he liked
the shape of the stone, probably because it was a female

stone. He had been lifting it every few days, whenever the urge became irresistible, and nothing was going to stop him from doing it now, right out in the open.

At any rate, this prehistoric man did something historic. He lifted a woman. In order to do so, he put his arms around her middle, where she was smallest and easiest to get hold of. It was also, though he did not understand it in these terms, her center of gravity, about equal amounts of her being above and below, and front and rear.

The moment he put his arms around the woman and started to lift, the man knew he had something different on his hands. For one thing, the woman was amazingly light, compared to a stone of the same size. Also she was smoother, warmer, and several centuries younger than any stone he had ever lifted before. Moreover she moved, in an interesting way, and no stone he had lifted had moved in any way, except when he let go of it.

As he held her there, in this First Embrace, her face was opposite his and her toes dangled against his shins. The upper front of her, in two parts, was pressed against the upper part of his upper front and was soft, but not too soft. She smiled and put her arms around his shoulders to keep herself from falling if he should let go, having spied a stone he preferred to lift.

But, to quote from Wordsworth's "Michael," which is something the Stone Age man could not have done, after that experience he "never lifted up a single stone." Or a double one, either. He was through with stones, except for crushing the heads of other Stone Age men who tried to lift his woman.

A short time later he learned that different women, like different stones, are of different sizes around the middle, have more or less sticking out in front and back, and react differently to being lifted. He did quite a bit of experimenting, and almost had his own head crushed several times.

In the end, and there is some dispute about which end, he learned that it was not necessary to lift a woman, especially a tall woman, when putting his arm around her.

The embrace, which was to play such a large part in bringing men and women together, was born.

The Classical Period

The embrace flourished in ancient Greece and Rome, though there were some who objected to embracing in Greece, considering it a perversion or beneficial only to those with dry skin. Despite the evidence of some statues, the Greeks had two arms, just like later peoples, and were quite capable of embracing.

During the Golden Age in Greece, everything was golden. Even silence was golden—one of the greatest achievements of classical goldsmiths. Since Greek women wore a golden belt around their waist, known as the golden mean, they were somewhat protected when they were hard pressed. But Greek warriors, aware of this, carried swords with which to cut the Gordian knot or anything else that got in their way. Gold, after all, is a soft metal, and the Greeks were hard men and not easily thwarted.

Of all the Greek women, Helen was the most beautiful. It was shortly after she was voted The Women I Would Most Like to Embrace that Paris, son of the king of Troy, seduced her and carried her away. That left her husband, Menelaus, with nothing to put his arms around but Greek pillars. There were many of these, but despite their number and variety (Doric, Ionic, and Corinthian), Menelaus never could find one that felt like Helen. So he led the Greeks against the Trojans in a ten-year war to get her back (and all the rest of her).

As for the popularity of embracing among the Trojans, Virgil has written a long poem about this, opening "Arms and the man I sing." What he had in mind was a man's arms and how he has an irrepressible urge to put them around a woman, especially a woman like Helen.

The Greeks, a curious lot, embraced not only women but ideas. The latter is the sort of thing that gives satisfaction only to a philosopher. As a matter of fact, we are told that "some embraced Plato and some embraced Aristotle," which indicates that these two gentlemen appealed to other men, at least intellectuals, in a rather irregular way. While men were embracing Plato and Aristotle, there is no telling what was happening to their wives, at home.

Among the Romans, embracing went forward vigorously, especially at orgies. Sometimes a Roman would embrace a woman while he was eating, holding onto her through seven or eight courses. That is why Romans usually ate lying on a couch. While they embraced, a man and a woman would do all sorts of sensuous and decadent things, such as feeding each other grapes and figs. It was overeating, as well as overembracing, that led to the decline and fall of the Roman Empire and made Edward Gibbon famous.

Probably the greatest embracer among the Romans was Julius Caesar, who went all the way to Egypt to put his arms around Cleopatra and thought it was worth it. Night after night he drove Cleopatra around in his chariot, parking in the back of a pyramid. According to some accounts, he was able to hold the reins of his spirited horses in one hand and put the other hand around Cleopatra's waist, it was that small. It was quite a sight, according to Suetonius and others who did not see it.

The only impediment to embracing, among the Romans, was the toga. This loose garment with no waist-line made it difficult to determine where to put the arms around. Any visual appraisal being inaccurate, it was necessary to feel here and there to find the place. This often took quite a bit of valuable time that might otherwise have gone into embracing.

The Middle Ages

If the toga was something of a nuisance to the ancient Romans, think of what a suit of armor meant to men of the Middle Ages. Of course a man might take off his armor and chain mail and all the rest, or nearly all the rest, before embracing a woman. But sometimes he couldn't wait, and the woman was badly scraped and bruised. She could even be scarred for life, especially if, in his haste, the man failed to put down his pike and halberd.

Or the damsel could have her front teeth knocked out if he forgot to pull up his visor.

It was fortunate, however, that in the Middle Ages women did not also wear suits, or dresses, of armor. There was only male mail, and not female mail. Had both sexes gone around clad in iron, the clash and clatter of even a gentle embrace would have been heard throughout and would have brought the servants in, gawking.

Serfs were lucky in that they did not wear armor, their lives not being considered worth protecting. They could therefore embrace at will, without fear of leaving telltale dents or spots of rust.

At medieval tournaments, knights jousted for the right to embrace some fair lady. Before the jousting began, the lady might drop her handkerchief as a sign of her favor. Should he fail in the tournament, a disappointed suitor might get a kick out of closing his eyes and embracing his horse. He might, in fact, get quite a kick out of this if his horse didn't go in for that sort of thing.

Often after rescuing a damsel who was being distressed by a dragon, a knight would carry her away on his horse, embracing her the while. Usually it was she who embraced him, trying to keep from falling off the horse as he galloped back to King Arthur. When he arrived at the court, as likely as not King Arthur was not there to congratulate him, being out trying to catch Lancelot or some other unfaithful faithful knight in the act of embracing Queen Guinevere. The knights sat at a round table and each took his turn.

Embracing was widely practiced in the part of the Middle Ages known as the Dark Ages, when people did all sorts of things they wouldn't have done in broad daylight.

The Modern Era

Embracing continued to be popular in Europe through the Renaissance, which was a period of enlightenment when even the more stupid began to catch on about a Good Thing. There was also a broadening of horizons, though women for the most part, and in the right parts, remained slender enough for a man's arms to go around and even overlap. (They overlapped over the lap when the woman was facing outward.) However, as Robert Browning was to say later, in his lines of encouragement to men trying to embrace fat women, "A man's reach should exceed his grasp." Since Elizabeth Barrett was thin and bony, it took a poet to appreciate the difficulties of others.

In France, at the time of Louis XIV and Louis XV, men wore lace cuffs and carried large handkerchiefs up their sleeves, and you might have thought it hard to tell whom to embrace. That is, until you saw Madame de

Pompadour or Madame du Barry, and then you realized that lace cuffs do not a woman make, and that the feminine in a woman keeps bobbing up, especially in a low-cut dress.

Embracing took an interesting turn at the time of Napoleon, who made two important contributions. First, he had to stand on a box to embrace Josephine, or to sit on his horse. Some scholars think he remained on his horse not to gain the necessary height but because by comparison with the horse Josephine was fairly attractive. Second, Napoleon made a great contribution to the technique of embracing by doing it with one hand. He kept the other nonchalantly tucked inside his coat. For pointing the way (with whichever hand was available), Napoleon is owed a debt of gratitude by all young men who today embrace with one hand while driving at seventy miles an hour with the other. His dreams of empire may have been shattered at Waterloo, but he left something more significant for which he will be remembered by posterity.

There was a parallel development in Germany, where young men in beer halls learned to hoist a stein with one hand and embrace a plump *Fräulein* with the other, without losing a teaspoonful of suds. Dancing the waltz, however, the young German clutched the girl with both hands, unless he was so experienced and skillful that he could cavort one-handed, meanwhile crying out disdainfully to others, in German, "Two hands for beginners!"

In Italy and Spain the embrace was downgraded, coming to be nothing more than a greeting. At the same time, to show how little it meant, men kissed women on the cheeks, first one side and then the other, as though they had tried for the mouth but missed. With the embrace and the kiss thus relegated to the level of the handshake (though the kiss continued to be a couple of feet higher, as a general rule), the passionate Latins had to find something more satisfying than the embrace, and they did.

In America, where the embrace was introduced by Sir Walter Raleigh, who had learned its finer points from Queen Elizabeth, it made rapid strides, except in Puritan New England. There, to embrace a friendly churchgoer was a sin worse than death, and to embrace an unfriendly Indian meant losing one's scalp, which was almost as bad. Any man caught embracing was stuck in the stocks, while any woman caught in the act was forced to wear a scarlet "E" on her bosom.

In Revolutionary times, patriots were too busy fighting the British to think much about embracing. Some of Washington's men suddenly thought about it, during that cold winter at Valley Forge, when it would have been a way to warm their hands. But the idea no sooner popped into their heads than they remembered that their wives and sweethearts were not available. A few hardy soldiers, especially those who had been minutemen, which meant that they were always prepared to embrace on a minute's notice, made snow women and tried to embrace them. Watching his men in the bitter cold, their sleeves frozen fast to a pile of snow, General Washington felt so deeply for them that tears came into his eyes. As they fell, they formed beautiful icicles, or in this instance eyecicles. Seldom in all history have embraces been so unsatisfactory and women so frigid.

And so we come to the present, when there is talk of automation taking over the embrace, along with everything else. To save effort, men will soon have robots to do their embracing for them. But lest you grow concerned about metal monsters that hug women to death, you should know that women will soon have robots to receive the embraces of men's robots.

Then men and women, lying cozily together, will push

the appropriate buttons and get a vicarious thrill out of listening to the whirring of gears and the clanking of metal against metal.

"That's us," he will say tenderly to her. And then, exhausted from the effort of watching and listening, they will both drop off to sleep.

AFTERTHOUGHT:

There are those who use the word "hug" instead of "embrace." Claudio, for instance, in *Measure for Measure,* says:

> I will encounter darkness as a bride,
> And hug it in mine arms.

Any man who can hug a hunk of darkness, pretending it is a gorgeous girl he has just married, has to have a vivid imagination and be an ingenious mime.

Much as I admire Shakespeare, when it comes to hugging I prefer the enthusiasm and flesh-and-blood quality of Ezra Pound's lines:

> Let him rebuke who ne'er has known the pure Platonic grapple,
> Or hugged two girls at once behind the chapel.

I like the "two girls at once," especially for a man who has long arms. And having first hugged girls (one at a time) behind the barn, I can see that to have done it behind a chapel would have made it a little naughtier and therefore more exciting.

Whether you call it an embrace or a hug, it brings people together.

The Typewriter and I

They say that the invention of gunpowder in the Middle Ages made the peasant the equal of the noble. With a gun in his hand, a peasant could make his liege lord do his bidding, such as stop fooling around with his wife, if his hand didn't shake too much.

Well, invention of the typewriter made me the equal of people who can write legibly. My handwriting may be undecipherable, but when I hit a key on my typewriter, the letter appears on the paper (assuming I have remembered to put in a piece of paper) as nice as can be. I may not be able to type as fast as a professional typist, but I can type as neatly, if I am careful.

Back in 1930 I bought a secondhand portable typewriter at the Harvard Cooperative Store, in Cambridge, for twenty-five dollars. For twenty-five cents I bought a manual entitled *How to Learn to Type in Ten Easy Lessons*. The manual told me where to put my fingers and provided ten typing exercises. After completing the ten exercises, I embarked upon the typing of my doctoral dissertation, which ran to nine hundred pages, in triplicate. When I had finished this task, carting off no telling how many reams of paper in my wastebasket, I was a fair typist.

Now I have five typewriters: a standard elite, a standard pica, a portable elite, a portable pica, and a lightweight typewriter to carry when traveling. The pica is for manuscripts and the elite is for correspondence. The reason I have two of each is that I have one at my office at the college and one at home. My wife thinks I need only one typewriter, the lightweight, because I am a lightweight writer.

Over the years I have come down from the use of ten fingers to eight, the little finger of each hand somehow having dropped out of the race, but I have learned to cross one hand over the other, like a piano virtuoso. Most professional typists can't do this, and I can't do it either if I stop to think of it. It reminds me of the old story of the centipede who was asked which foot he used first, and when he thought about it he got into a tangle and was immobilized. Anyhow, though my method is unorthodox, I bang along at quite a clip.

I used to write a draft longhand, and then type it off. But now I start right in at the typewriter. Except for verse. Verse I usually start longhand, but I shift over to the typewriter when I have the lines flowing. My handwriting demands this. It is such a miserable scrawl that I sometimes cannot decipher what I have just written. Also, writing by hand is much slower, and I haven't the patience for it any more.

My typewriters are all old, and I bought all but one of them secondhand. The reason one typewriter was bought new is that I bought it for my daughter when she was in college and complained about her old typewriter (which also was new) because it was elite type. She discovered that using small type required her to write term papers with about twenty percent more words in order to produce the same number of pages as students who used pica type. So I bought her this new one with pica type, but about that time she got married and dropped out of college and never used it. I repossessed it, this being about the only thing I could salvage, not being interested in her textbooks and pennants.

One reason I keep these old typewriters is that I am superstitious. I am afraid if I had new typewriters I would not write as well. Or perhaps I should say I would write more poorly. I feel the need to wrestle with a slightly balky typewriter, pausing now and then to untangle a couple of keys or reroll a ribbon that has bunched up. If everything went too smoothly, I might miss the physical part of writing. I think of writing as a constant battle between my typewriter and me. The typewriter is my antagonist, my competitor, but also my companion. To use a new typewriter or, still worse, to use an electric typewriter or a dictating machine, would be like playing a round of golf all by myself. It might spare me some distraction, playing golf in a onesome, but it would be a lonely sport, without competition or companionship. The same would be true, I think, of writing with a gadget having no personality and offering no resistance.

The typewriter I mostly use, especially for manuscripts, is about fifteen years old. I know its every virtue (chiefly durability) and its every vice (the squeaks that no oil will silence, the screws that keep loosening, the sly way the lever slips from double space to single space, the occasional and unpredictable failure of the shift lock to lock, which means that capitals come out lower case—and so on). My typewriter is almost human. I know its whims and vagaries as well as I know my wife's or my children's. We are growing old together, and I suspect we shall collapse together, on the same day—I hope when the last page of a book has been written rather than somewhere in the middle. I am thinking of asking that it be buried with me. Or we can be recycled together into something useful.

I have typed all of my magazine pieces and books myself. That includes all of the revisions, and I usually rewrite and completely retype a book from three to five times. Only twice, as I recall, have I turned over a book manuscript to a typist, a manuscript I had already retyped several times. In each instance I was busy typing the first draft of another book.

There are good reasons, aside from saving on typing bills, for my typing not only the first draft but all the revisions. For one thing, if I were to hand over to a typist my first version, with all the words crossed out and all the words written in between the lines and out into the margins, the typist would keep pestering me to tell her whether a word goes here or there, and what this word is that she can't quite make out, and whether I really meant to say thus and so. While she was asking me, I could be typing the thing myself.

There is another and more important reason for my do-it-yourself technique. A typist would bring the manuscript back to me exactly as I wrote it, except for any mistakes she made. There would be no editing, no improvement. On the other hand, when I type it myself I make changes as I go along, thinking of better words, better phrases, better ideas. Much as I may already have revised, I still revise during each typing. And even if these revisions are small, they add up to a significant total.

Of course habit plays a large part in writing, as it does in every kind of activity. The way I lean over my typewriter, the feel of the keys, the click of the key against paper, the tinkle of the margin bell, the scrape of the roller being pulled across for a new line, and the satisfying look of words popping up on the white paper—these are, to me, essential concomitants of the writing process. I would find it difficult to write, or to think (since I think while I write), without them.

Sometimes I feel I am, like those mythical creatures of old, half man and half something else, in this instance half typewriter. But I am not sure which half is which.

AFTERTHOUGHT:

As I have said, I own five typewriters. Until a few years ago, this was not so. Then there was an article about me in *The Christian Science Monitor,* called "Man with Five Typewriters." At the time I had only four, but the writer of the article wrote so pleasantly about me that I thought I should make an honest man of him. So I bought another.

My greatest trouble with typing is that the keys are always clogging up. To ream them out, I keep alongside my typewriter a large safety pin, always open and ready. The bit of inky lint I extract on the point of the pin I wipe off on a dark flower that is part of the design of the rug under my typewriter stand. As time goes by, this flower is getting darker and darker. My wife has noticed this and it puzzles her. She thinks it must have something to do with the effect of my study light on the dyestuff. I have no intention of explaining.

It is a great convenience to be able to lean over, after unclogging a clogged "a," wipe the pin back and forth, and then straighten up, ready to go to work on a rather fuzzy "g." Back in the days before ballpoint pens, I had a penwiper. What I need now and have, thanks to that rug, is a pinwiper.

The Conversation Game
and How to Win It

I have always wanted to be a good conversationalist—
the most sought-after guest at a social gathering, the
person everyone rushes to sit next to at the dinner
table.

"Oh, that darling man," I have hoped dowagers and
their well-endowed daughters would say to me. "What
profundity! What wit! I could listen to him for hours."

There was a time when I prepared for each dinner
party. I read the latest books. I saw the latest movies and
plays. I memorized lines of poetry. I kept notes on funny
stories I heard, and practiced telling them in front of a
mirror to get just the right intonation and gestures as I
led up to the hilarious climax.

But, honestly, I was never much of a success. Someone
else always stole the show. At the dinner table, I tried in
vain to hold the attention of those around me, or even

127

the person next to me, with well-informed comments on the world situation, appropriate lines from Tennyson and T. S. Eliot, or a story that had doubled me up when I heard it. But before the first course was served, my partner usually became engaged in conversation with the person on the other side of her, and her only words to me until we got up from the table were, "Would you please pass the salt?"

Then, one day, everything changed. Overnight I became the prize of every dinner party.

"You *must* let me sit by you," beautiful ladies gushed. "I understand you are simply fascinating." It was almost embarrassing, the way I was pursued by those who had previously ignored me. I began to feel sorry for the handsome, brilliant young men who were passed by in the mad scramble to gain a coveted position by my side.

I know precisely when the turning point came in my career as a conversationalist. I was at a dinner party I almost declined because I had such a bad attack of laryngitis. My voice was completely gone. When I tried to speak, all that issued forth was a mournful croak. I resigned myself to an evening of isolation, planning to excuse myself early to go home and take the pills prescribed by my doctor.

At the dinner table I was seated between two ladies, both of whom, on previous occasions, I had tried unsuccessfully to dazzle, or even to maintain small talk with. When they saw they were seated next to me, they tried to hide their disappointment, but the gaiety went out of their eyes. They seemed to be thinking, "What did I do to deserve this?"

Though she would obviously have preferred to talk with the person on the other side of her, the lady on my right felt compelled to drop a few polite words in my direction before turning away from me for the rest of the evening.

"Have you ever known such a rainy season as we have been having?" she asked.

"Mm-m," I said. I wanted to tell her about that day in 1958, when it rained four inches in two hours and within a week we had had a third of our annual average rainfall. Then I wanted to say that this was really nothing, because in Cherrapunji, India, in July, 1861, a world record of 366.14 inches of rain fell in a single month. But all I could do was point at my throat and smile wanly.

"You poor dear," she said. "You have a terrible case of laryngitis. But you will get your voice back in no time if you follow my advice. Have you an ice bag?"

"Awrk," I said.

"Then you must put a cold compress on your throat for at least ten minutes every hour. It drives the congestion out."

At this point the lady on my left became interested in our conversation. "Do I understand you have laryngitis?" she asked.

I nodded, at the same time looking pathetic.

"I know just the thing for it," she said. "Breathe steam from a teakettle. It will loosen the membranes."

For a while the two ladies argued back and forth about the merits of their respective cures. Then, while the lady on my left was momentarily and reluctantly drawn into conversation with someone else, the lady on my right asked me, "Have you seen any good movies lately?"

"Awrk," I said.

"Oh," she said, "I forgot about your laryngitis. Now you just rest your throat." Thereupon she related the plot of the latest "adult" movie she had seen, with critical comments on the acting ability of the stars and supporting cast of each, followed by a heated attack on the motion-picture industry for its lowering of moral standards.

Instead of asking her why she went to see these sex-obsessed movies she deplored, as I might have done had I my voice, I managed a concerned look which she apparently took for agreement. Having exhausted the subject of motion pictures, she gave me a vigorous critique of what she called "the situation in Washington." This she followed with a full account of her childhood, her courtship, her travels, and her three children. From time to time, as the situation required, I nodded, shook my head, or got off a sympathetic "Awrk."

"Can't I get in on this interesting conversation?" the lady on my left asked playfully but a little petulantly. No sooner had I turned my face slightly in her direction than she was off on her hobby: growing orchids. She told me about the different species, cross-breeding, the problems of humidity control, and dozens of other things in which I had no interest whatsoever. But since I had no voice, I was unable to change the subject. She went on and on, mistaking my sleepy nods for indications of fascination and agreement.

Shortly after we left the table, I happened to overhear my two dinner companions talking to each other.

"He is the most exciting man," I heard the lady who had sat at my right say. "He knows something about everything."

"Yes," said the lady who had sat at my left, "I was amazed at how much he knows about orchids."

Eventually I got over my laryngitis. But I had learned the secret of a good conversationalist: the ability to keep quiet.

There is more to it than that. A great deal of skill is involved. An "Awrk" is not enough, especially when you haven't laryngitis. Nor are "Yes" and "No" sufficient or, at times, desirable. More effective are such indications of interest and such prompting words and phrases as "You don't say!" "Go on, go on," "Do you really mean that?"

"Well, I declare!" "That's something I must remember," "Where do you get all your information?" (or "You must read a lot"), and "Really!"

"Really!" is perhaps the best multi-purpose word. It interrupts the speaker for only a second, if at all, and it can be used over and over. Much depends, of course, upon the way it is said. Spoken with a rising inflection, it indicates interest, even excitement; with a falling inflection, sympathy. Spoken sharply and quickly, it indicates a sharing of annoyance or disgust. Long drawn out, it gives evidence of thoughtfulness, meditation. For an all-around response, nothing else is quite so useful.

Sounds can be interspersed among words, or substituted for them, with good effect. Thus a low whistle is almost the exact equivalent of a long "Really!" Accompanied by a slight squinting of the eyes, it can mean either shrewdness or the sensing of a tight situation. A quick, high whistle, more of a chirp, is excellent for indicating surprise. A wolf whistle, amidst or at the end of a sexy story, shows appreciation and fellow feeling among males.

The snapping of fingers is a good way to show the person talking to you that you are all keyed up about what he is saying and can hardly wait for him to get on. Since I myself am not good at snapping my fingers, I have come to substitute quick, nervous taps on the table with my knuckles or, when these have taken about all they can stand, a pen or pencil. In any case, the person to whom I am listening knows that I am right in there and not missing a word.

Of course neither words nor sounds are absolutely necessary. A great deal can be done simply with facial expressions. I have mentioned squinting. The opposite, opening the eyes wide, to show the whites, is an excellent way of expressing amazement or fright, especially the latter. It must not be overdone, of course, or it will frighten the person who is talking. At first, the muscles of my eyelids being unaccustomed to sustained effort, I could show the whites of my eyes for only a few seconds without strain. Now, however, I can open my eyes to the full and hold them that way for several minutes while listening to gruesome details about an automobile accident, or even one that "almost happened."

Wrinkling the forehead and knitting the brows are equally effective means of revealing worry and perturbation. In fact, though this will be found difficult at first, with practice the two can be managed simultaneously. Lifting the eyebrows denotes either surprise or skepticism. Twitching the nose, or causing a slight flaring of the nostrils, can be used to indicate sympathetic distaste or anger.

The mouth is by far the most mobile and therefore the most versatile part of the face when it comes to making encouraging signals to the person to whom you are listening. Dropping the jaw and opening the mouth wide is one of the easiest ways I have discovered to look spellbound. More subtle is pursing the lips, perhaps simultaneously lifting the eyebrows and wrinkling the forehead to show the very deepest and fiercest concentration. Tightening the lips, meanwhile sticking out the tongue a trifle (not too far) has much the same effect. So also biting the lower lip or, for variety, the upper lip.

While doing any of these things, it is important to look the speaker directly in the eye. Otherwise one may achieve exactly the opposite of the desired effect: the listener may seem to be (1) thinking of something else or (2) desperately contriving some means of escape. One person of my acquaintance, who should get along brilliantly as a conversationalist, spoils everything by looking away as if his mind is on other things. No amount of saying "Really!" and biting the lips does any good. By not keeping his eyes on the person talking to him, he is rated a poor conversationalist, despite all his other skills, by those who talk to him.

The only bad thing, now that I have learned how to be a sought-after conversationalist, is that my mind is going to pot. Instead of preparing myself by reading the latest books and going to movies, plays, and concerts, all I do now is listen. Of course I might learn something if I really listened, but now, you see, I know how to listen without hearing. Or to hear without listening.

Anyhow, I get more dinner invitations than I can possibly accept. And while beautiful ladies are busy talking to me, and I am seemingly listening with my new-found skill, I can give all my attention to looking them over. I am interested, all right, but not in what they are saying.

AFTERTHOUGHT:

Back in my publish-or-perish days I wrote a book, in collaboration with Raymond F. Howes, called *Coleridge the Talker*. It served its purpose. Instead of perishing, I was promoted.

A reviewer of the book said that the three greatest talkers of all times were, in chronological order, Socrates, Christ, and Coleridge. This put our man in good company, apparently a cut above such tongue-waggers as Samuel Johnson and Oscar Wilde.

Most talkers are not, however, conversationalists. They are monologists, or monopolists. Sometimes they are also monotonists. If they are good at it, they become lecturers and are paid for it. If they aren't good at it, they are avoided. Among the married couples I know, usually one person is a talker and the other is a listener. Sometimes the husband is the talker. Sometimes, and more often, it is the wife. Only rarely, in my experience, do talkers or listeners marry each other. Of the various combinations, the worst is two talkers. Since it is nerve-wracking and almost unbearable to outsiders, what must it be like, day after day, to the two participants? Could they possibly have known about this before they married?

Despite what I have written about how to be rated a good conversationalist, I am a congenital talker. I inherited the tendency from my father, who inherited it from his mother. That is as far back as I have been able to trace this weakness, or over-strength. How I wish I had inherited, instead, something really useful, such as straight teeth, good eyesight, or money.

There are far more talkers than listeners in the world, at least in the part of the world I know. If you are a listener, you are lucky. You are sure to be successful, or at any rate popular.

"Lend me your ears," you often hear someone say, at the same time borrowing the words of Shakespeare's Mark Antony. But tell me, please, did you ever hear anyone say, "Lend me your mouth"?

For kissing, maybe, but not for talking.

Reading for a
Desert Island

The next time I am asked what book I would like to have if I were marooned on a desert island, I know my choice. It would be the *New English Dictionary* (1888–1933). Running to eleven huge volumes of small print, it would last me a long time, perhaps until someone picked up my note in an empty cough-syrup bottle and sent out a rescue party. The *NED* is crammed with fascinating information not usually included in a dictionary. In addition to the usual meanings and etymologies, it quotes from works dating back hundreds of years, and thus combines lexicography and history.

Recently I opened the M-N volume, thinking to look up the word "medical." I already knew the ordinary things about the word, such as its coming from the Latin *medicus*, physician, and being akin to *mederi*, to heal, and *remedium*, remedy. I also knew that it can be traced

back to the Greek names of healing deities such as *Medos,*
and to the Greek *medea,* plans, counsels, arts, and the
Latin *meditari,* to think over, to practice, whence comes
our word "meditate." But I thought the *NED* might have
some less obvious information, and I was right. Let me
share with you a few of my discoveries.

Take the word "medic," today a colloquial, slangy
word for physician or medical student. This was not always so. Back in 1659 T. Pecke could write in all serious-
ness, and nearly all capitals, "The Medic heals the Body."
And the Calvinist preacher Jonathan Edwards used the
word in serious writing (the only kind, for him), but
spelled it "medick."

Then consider the word "medicable," meaning capable
of being cured. This, which the *NED* quotes from works
as far back as 1616, was once used much more freely than
today. Wordsworth, for instance, mindful of the carnage
at Waterloo, caused its syllables to roll out mellifluously
in his lines:

> For those who stood unhurt, or bled
> With medicable wounds.

Today we would send in helicopters and men to stop the
bleeding, and whisk the wounded to a rear area.

As for "medicament," Thackeray uses it in *Pendennis,*
telling us that one of his characters "had been treated and
medicamented as the doctor ordained," which at any rate
is better than being left out on the battlefield to bleed to
death. And W. Barclay, writing back in 1614, stakes his
reputation on the fact that "Tobacco is the only medicament in the world ordained by nature to entertaine good
companie." Obviously he had not read the Surgeon General's report.

Passing over "medicamental," "medicamentary," and
"medicamentous," we come to "medicaster," a pretender

to medical skill, which somehow seems a nicer word to use than our modern and rather blunt "quack." It can be found as early as 1602, in a work where it is spelled "medicastra," giving a hint that the poor fellow had, perhaps unwillingly, undergone surgery. The medical profession knew how to take care of unqualified practitioners in those days.

To "medicate" was not always to add health-giving medicinal substances. In 1662, with a suggestion that even in those days cities had their problems with air pollution, a writer remarked that "the Fumes, Steams, and Stenches of London do so medicate and impregnate the Air about it that. . . ." And in 1684 there was a reference to rather inhospitable hosts who "medicate their Wines with Arsenick and Mercury."

We can go all the way back to 1298 with "medicinable," and an interesting bit of bandaging (and spelling) can be found in a work published in 1425: "Hee bonde uppe hir legge with medecynnabil clothes." A writer in 1577 tells us that "Cow milk is most medicinable," while Shakespeare in *Othello* uses the word figuratively and poetically in "Drop tears as fast as the Arabian trees their medicinable gum." At one time physicians wore, on the fourth finger of either hand, a medicinable ring, a ring that had been blessed and was supposed to have curative powers. This finger therefore came to be known as the "medicinable" (or "medicable" or "medical") finger, a fact that might be of interest to proctologists.

The *NED* cites the word "medicine" in the *Ancren Riwle* as early as 1225, the word in those days often being connected with necromancy, magic, elixirs, potions, and the philosopher's stone. Modern makers of beauty creams would, I am sure, like to unearth the formula referred to in 1555, when a writer tells us that "they anoint their body and their face with certain medicines, whereby they

become slick and smoothe." Then again, "medicine" was
used in 1651 in a rather uncomplimentary reference to
physicians as "medicine-mongers."

One more item. In a supplementary volume, the *NED*
includes the term "medicine ball." I find a reference in
1903 to "passing medicine balls," but since this was in a
sports magazine, it could hardly refer to something like
kidney stones.

Now you see why I want the *New English Dictionary,*
all eleven volumes, on that desert island. With reading
matter such as it contains, and with the world in its present shape, I might spurn—yes, even fight off—any attempts to rescue me.

AFTERTHOUGHT:

My love of a dictionary can hardly be overstated. When
I am sick, I take a dictionary rather than a detective
thriller to bed with me. A dictionary *is* a thriller. I am
never sure what strange word or undreamed-of etymology
I may encounter on the next page—or in the footnotes,
among the archaic and obsolete terms that fascinate me
most. Fortunately, I have never had to choose between
a dictionary and my wife. It would not be easy.

One of our Presidents, Millard Fillmore, was the son of
a poor farmer. He grew up in a home in which there was
not a single book. Not until he was nineteen did he buy a
book for himself. That first book was a dictionary. I have
always thought it was this choice that marked him out for
the Presidency. Of course he was not a great President.
Maybe he should have bought a book earlier or, when he
was nineteen, two books. Anyhow, Fillmore, who went to
school very little, married his teacher, a nice example of
Instant Education. I don't know how she looked, but she
must have had a good library.

Every Day Is
Father's Day

The other day I did a little research on the word "father." Having been one for thirty years, I thought it high time to know what I am. Everyone is aware that "father" is related to the Latin *pater,* but perhaps everyone doesn't know that it is also akin to "patriarch," "patrician," and "patriot." Nice words, all of them.

What pleased me most was the discovery that "father" has an etymological connection with "Jupiter," literally the "sky father."

My kinship with Jupiter bucked me up considerably. Not wishing to let my ancestor down, I began to take a more lordly attitude around the house. No more helping with the dishes. No more giving in when our son begs to use the family car, his own having something serious the matter with it, such as being out of gas. No more watching my wife's favorite television program instead of mine.

"What's got into you?" my wife asked. "Are you sick or something?"

I told her about my being related to Jupiter. I thought this might improve my status a little, but she shrugged it off.

"Oh, for heaven's sake!" she said, handing me a dish towel. "You'd better put on your apron if you don't want to get all messed up."

So I soon got Jupiter out of my mind and went back to being an ordinary father.

As a matter of fact an ordinary father, the kind I am, isn't good enough. I would like to be an extraordinary father. If I could go back thirty years and start all over with our son, or go back twenty-eight years and start all over with our daughter, I know some improvements I would make.

The main thing I would do would be to give my children more of my time. As an ordinary father, I gave my children about the ordinary amount of time. But that's not enough. Now I wish I had subtracted time from my personal pleasures or my work and given it to them.

I gave them a fair amount of time around the house. I helped them (occasionally too much) with their homework. I talked with them about their problems. I showed an interest in the things they were interested in. But I wish I had given my weekends and, during summer vacations, whole weeks to the exploration of nature with them. We lived near the mountains and not far from the desert and the sea, but I never took them on a camping trip, never taught them how to pitch a tent or light a fire or catch a fish or collect geological specimens or look up at the heavens and identify the stars.

Aside from being a little too selfish about the use of my time, there is a very good reason why I did none of these things. Frankly, I don't know how to pitch a tent, I can't light a fire without using a whole box of matches, and the only time I ever went fishing I made a wild cast and snagged my cheek with the hook. I never studied geology, so I can't tell one rock from another, and the extent of my knowledge about the stars is my ability, after a few false starts, to identify the Big Dipper.

Perhaps I was discouraged about nature by my father, who took the family camping exactly twice before he gave up forever. The first time, he was cooking some beans over a campfire when his wool shirt caught on fire. My mother and I stood by helplessly while he rolled in the dirt and put it out. We were so shaken by the experience that there was no more fun the rest of the trip. The second time, my grandmother went along and my father slammed the car door on her hand and almost cut off two of her fingers. The rest of *that* trip was no lark either.

I am envious of fathers who know about flora and fauna and rocks and fish and stars, and who lead the way to nature. Ignorant as I was, I might have learned something, and while doing so could have been with my wife and children under conditions that would have drawn us closer together. Instead, my humiliating weakness with regard to nature persisted, as I once expressed it in the following lines:

> When I consider flowers,
> I must admit I'm silly,
> For I can't tell an aster
> From a calla lily.
> I can't identify
> An iris or a peony,
> And if I had to grow them
> There simply wouldn't be any.

In another area, however, I have done better. And this is an important one too. I mean reading aloud. As soon as

my children would listen, which was very soon, I read
poems and stories to them. When they were small, I read
aloud for a half hour or an hour before they went to bed,
and then often for another half hour after they were
tucked in. When they were older, right up through high
school and college, I often brought a magazine or a book
to the table to read. My wife was not sure this was good
for our digestion, and she knew it was bad table manners,
but I persisted.

For many years I have had a large unabridged dictionary on a stand with rollers on the four legs. Many a time
to settle an argument (especially when I was sure I was
right) I have wheeled it in to the dining room table and
read off a meaning or a pronunciation or an etymology.

So if I failed my children by not sharing nature with
them, I did better about books. And I suggest to all parents—both fathers and mothers—a return to the old-
fashioned pleasure of reading aloud. Not only will children and parents learn something from the treasure trove
of books, but also the family will be drawn closer together
by the experience.

There is another thing to be said for reading aloud, a
practice almost abandoned today. Children will start out
by hearing words as well as seeing them. They will make
the delightful discovery that words have more than meaning. They have lightness and heaviness, thickness and
thinness, roughness and smoothness. Children have a
natural liking for words, and this can be cultivated and
built upon if there are always plenty of books around the
house and if there is some reading aloud. Think of how
the smallest child can triumphantly reel off "supercali-
fragilisticexpialidocious," while I, with my slow brain
and slower tongue, can never manage to get past the first
four or five syllables.

Having spent a large part of my life reading books,
teaching from them, reviewing them, and writing them, I

don't think I am overemphasizing the importance of books in the home. I remember the wonderful experience I had with a book when my children were twelve and ten, and we were living in Paris, and I read to them, a chapter a day, from Dickens' *A Tale of Two Cities.* The only thing better than reading a good book is reading it aloud to someone.

Of course some fathers turn the reading aloud over to their wives, or to Grandfather or Grandmother. There is a good chance that grandparents go back to that earlier time when reading aloud in the home was a regular thing. So they can do it unself-consciously and with gusto. Packed away in my own freight of recollections are memories of being read to by my grandmother and even by my great-grandmother.

I began by telling of my discovery of the etymological connection between "father" and "Jupiter," and my brief glorying in playing head god in our family. In truth, I sincerely believe that the father should be head of the house. I think he should have the final word, and I believe most wives and children prefer it that way. But I also think a man should wield his authority gently and considerately and should whenever possible back up his wife's rulings and suggestions concerning the children.

In our thirty-nine years of marriage, the only quarrels between my wife and me were when I let her down in our dealings with our children. I was usually the weak one, the one who gave in, the one who said "Yes" when it should have been "No" or at least "Maybe." Occasionally I did something even worse. I said, "Ask your mother."

I think a father should have more spine than I have. At the same time, he should act cooperatively with his partner and not take unilateral, unsupported action. I know a father whose word is law in his household. His wife and children tremble when he speaks. In fact he scares *me* a little. If I am too weak, he is too strong. I get love from my children, but not much respect. He gets respect but not much love.

One thing that has helped our family through many minor crises has been our ability to see the ridiculousness of a situation and of our behavior. When we see that we have blown up some small issue too much, we laugh it down to proper size.

As I look back on thirty years of fatherhood, I see that I could have done better, but I also could have done worse. It is a little late for me to start over.

So my fatherly advice to fathers is: Give time, while there is time, to your children. Introduce them to nature and to books, and share these experiences with them. Be firm, but not stubborn. And keep your sense of humor alive.

AFTERTHOUGHT:

Since writing the above, I have become a grandfather. Though I am not yet ready to start giving advice to fellow grandfathers, I should guess that, with my propensity for advice-giving, it will not be long.

The main thing I have learned so far about being a grandfather is that it is easier. Usually the easier comes first. It's a pity you can't begin by being a grandfather and then become a father later, when you are ready for it. Nature is usually pretty good about such things. Notice how spring prepares you for summer and fall for winter. Courtship comes before marriage, too, and not after, except in rare cases. There seems to have been a little slip-up, however, in the father-grandfather sequence. Unfortunately, it's nothing you can remedy by legislation.

And So to Beds

What subject is more universal than beds? In beds most of us were conceived and born. In beds we spend a third of our lives, assuming we get eight hours sleep a night, and not counting any time we may spend in bed for purposes other than sleeping, such as reading a good book.

Beds are universal and timely. A recent study blames the use of twin beds (and excessively wide king-size beds) for an increase in the divorce rate. Attempts to fool around with the conventional shape of beds have also taken their toll. For instance a Hollywood actress, who has been married four times, insists on sleeping in a heart-shaped bed. Can you picture a man and a woman lying in a heart-shaped bed, with plenty of space at the top but no room for their feet? No wonder this actress's husbands kept leaving her, growing tired of playing footsies night after night.

"If the bed could tell all it knows, it would put many

to the blush," according to a seventeenth-century English proverb. Since beds aren't talking, unless they are bugged (with electronic bedbugs), I find it recumbent on me to tell all I know about beds. Admittedly, you would prefer to hear from a talking bed, but sometimes one has to take second best.

Literature is full of allusions to beds. There is Christopher Marlowe's "And I will make thee beds of roses" in *The Passionate Shepherd to his Love,* the shepherd being too passionate to think straight and to consider how and where a scratch by a thorn could be pretty painful. There is also Benjamin Franklin's:

> Early to bed and early to rise
> Makes a man healthy, wealthy, and wise.

And the revised version:

> Late to bed and early to rise
> Gives a man circles under his eyes.

There is the classic remark made in 1934 by Joe Jacobs, when he left a sickbed to go to Detroit to attend the World Series baseball game between Detroit and Chicago. He bet on Chicago, and Detroit won the series. "I should have stood in bed," was the memorable way Jacobs put it, hating to take it lying down. And then, to come to a contemporary literary figure, there is that gem of wisdom by the modern Confucius, Groucho Marx: "It isn't politics that makes strange bedfellows. It's matrimony." No one yet has coined the aphorism, "Beds make fellows strange" or "Strange beds make fellows. . . ." But someone will any day.

Speaking of strangeness and beds, it has always seemed strange to me that anyone would say, "You have made your bed, now lie in it." I think it should be, as I have more often heard it, "You have been lying there long enough. Now get up and make your bed." This would seem a more logical sequence.

History is replete with lore about beds. For instance, in England in the late eighteenth century there was a Dr. Graham, who offered the public what was technically called a Celestial Magnetico-Electrical Bed. This hymeneal couch was guaranteed to increase health and fertility. A childless couple could have a go at it, or in it, for five pounds sterling. Every part of the bed was said to be full of celestial and electric fire, as well as magnetic fluid, and at no extra cost a vocal solo "with the charms of an agreeable voice," could be heard in the background. Whether the soloist was paid anything, or took it out in looking through a peephole, is not known.

Quite the opposite of this stimulating bed, "calculated to give the necessary degree of strength and exertion to the nerves," was a certain herb used by the ancient Greeks. This was placed by Greek wives in their beds to keep them chaste when their husbands were away on business (such as fighting a small war) for as long as three or four days. The leaves of the herb, which were said to have a "refrigerating faculty," were most effective when the woman lay on her stomach, with the leaves under her. As long as the leaves stayed in place, she was safe. The husband must also have done something of the sort while he was away, because it is said that on departing he "took his leave." When he came home, bearing a crumpled leaf, his wife could be sure that he, too, had been faithful.

Beds have long been the place of business of many persons, and not only ladies of pleasure. In the seventeenth and eighteenth centuries kings received their courtiers at levees, signing decrees and papers of state while reclining in bed. Milton wrote most of *Paradise Lost* in bed, which may explain why the poem has put so many readers to sleep. And the composer Donizetti is said to have been so lazy that he rewrote a sheet of music rather than pick up his first draft, which had slipped off the bed.

According to Reginald Reynolds, in his authoritative work, *Beds,* a Spanish physician in the late nineteenth century grew so weary making house calls that he took to his bed and remained there for sixteen years, while his patients reversed the procedure and came to his bedside. He thus not only conserved his strength for his medical practice but avoided any criticism of his bedside manner, putting the responsibility on his patients.

The word "bed," as I should have explained at the outset, comes from the Anglo-Saxon *bedd,* and it will be noted that it was originally, as so many words of this origin still are, a four-letter word. "Bed," as in "flower bed," means a level plot of ground and is all right for flowers but hardly satisfactory for people unless they are in a hurry to lie down somewhere. Flowers are handicapped by their inability to go from one bed to another. The only way they can get around is by way of a third party, such as a bee. Bees go from bed to bed, carrying pollen, either trying to be helpful to bedfast flowers or getting their kicks vicariously.

The word "hotbed," by the way, has nothing to do with sex. Nor is a bedroll something you eat in bed.

Now let us take a look at some of the bed customs and costumes of history.

In the Stone Age, when men prepared a bed by leveling off part of the floor of their cave, removing the sharper stones, they never had anything, such as a coin or a cufflink, roll under the bed. Nor did they ever have to sweep under such a bed. The earliest pillow was probably a stone—as smooth and soft a stone as could be found. Most people in those days were sensible enough not to try to fluff up a stone pillow before resting their head on it.

Speaking of pillows, I have read that peasants in some parts of Europe sleep with their pillow under their feet rather than their head, explaining that their feet deserve it because they work harder. This is a very reasonable explanation, and if any other part of your body works harder than either your feet or your head, you might consider giving it the comfort it has earned.

According to the Golden Legend, St. Macarius of Alexandria dug up a dead pagan and used him as a pillow. The good saint was obviously trying to prove something, perhaps that the only good-for-something pagan is a dead pagan. At least Macarius was not bothered by feathers working loose and getting into his nostrils.

After the Stone Age, beds rapidly progressed from piles of straw and skins of animals to the feather bed (originally goose feathers, probably getting their name from people who slept on them in the raw), and thence to canopied beds, trundle beds, four-poster beds, and the Murphy bed. The Murphy bed was a bed that could be swung out of sight behind a door or into a closet. I know very little about Mr. Murphy, its inventor. But I do know that Murphy's button, named after J. B. Murphy, an American surgeon, is a device for reuniting two parts of an intestine after division. It could be that this ingenious doctor also invented the Murphy bed, so that he could combine his bedroom and his office and always be on the job, like the Spanish doctor mentioned above who never left his bed. But one lexicographer suggests that Murphy is a corruption of Morpheus, the god of sleep, and I rather like that. However, if Murphy is a corruption of Morpheus, perhaps Morpheus in turn is a corruption of Murphy, and the expression "in the arms of Morpheus" should actually be "in the arms of Murphy," Murphy being a virile and versatile Irishman who really got around, or at any rate got his arms around.

While beds were progressing toward our modern Hollywood bed, complete with mattress, innersprings, and starlet, there were important developments in bed attire.

Consider, for instance, the nightcap, which once warmed the head and now warms the stomach. Nightgowns were the principal attire, even for the unprincipled, for centuries. When pajamas came in, they were at first worn only by men. Then both men and women wore them, in an effort (that failed) to make the two sexes look exactly alike, especially in bed. One thing about pajamas that isn't true of nightgowns is that a quick pull at the end of the drawstring and the bottoms will drop down—unless the drawstring has not been tied in a bow, as it always should be. In that case the string will knot up and you may think you will *never* get those bottoms off, and may have to resort to a knife or a pair of scissors if you are in a hurry.

Whether to wear both tops and bottoms, only the tops, or only the bottoms has long been a serious problem. Economy would seem to dictate that the man would wear the tops and the woman the bottoms, or vice versa, in order to make one pair of pajamas do for two persons, with a considerable saving in wear and tear and laundry. In this connection, a recent statistical survey in France shows that one out of three Frenchmen does not wear pajamas, and twenty-eight percent of those who do, wear only one of two pieces. Though the survey does not indicate which of the two pieces is the more popular, and no comparable survey has yet been made in the United States, it led to composition of the lines that follow:

> Consider with what sacrifice,
>   What loss of time and sleep,
> The notebook-laden chap goes forth
>   At night to take a peep.
>
> For us, who calmly read results,
>   He travels far to Paris

And makes investigations which
　　You'd think might well embarrass.

He risks the gendarme on his beat,
　　The Frenchman with insomnia,
The ladder with a rotten rung,
　　The charge of Peeping Tomnia.

We'll not forget these hard-won facts,
　　The statistician's trade.
We also hope we'll not forget
　　Tonight to pull the shade.

Complete nudity in bed would seem to be the best solution if it is hard to decide whether to wear pajama tops or pajama bottoms. As for keeping warm, there is always the warming pad or the foot warmer, the best form of the latter being a brick heated in the oven and wrapped in a piece of flannel. The advantage of a heated brick over a hot-water bottle is obvious to anyone who has been in bed with a hot-water bottle that has sprung a leak.

Passing over (or under) that modern invention, the electric blanket, we come to that ancient but still much-used device, a human bed warmer in the form (and the nicer the form the better) of a companion. One of the curious scientific facts about warming a bed is that two persons in bed, although each has the same body temperature of 98.6 degrees, raise the temperature so much that it becomes necessary to throw off most of the bedclothes. No doubt an important physical principle is involved, and someone, like that statistician in France, will probably carry on research in this field. It is hoped that couples can be prevailed upon, in the interest of science, to lie together in bed while the researcher records the gradual rise in temperature and other physiological phenomena.

In this connection, reference should be made to a

French doctor, Charles de l'Orme, who kept his legs warm by wearing six pairs of stockings. It was easier to get a run in them than to run with them on.

Getting back to my main subject, let me now mention two of the most interesting of all beds, the Procrustean bed and the Bed of Ware. The Procrustean bed was the invention of a legendary highwayman of Attica who tied his victims on an iron bed. If their length exceeded that of the bed, he trimmed their legs down a bit; if the bed was too long, he stretched their legs until they fit. Lucky indeed was the person who was exactly the right size. Whether it would be more painful to have your legs cut off just above the ankle or stretched six inches or so is a moot point, and you should be glad not to have to put it to the test. If you are too long for a bed, say in a hotel, the worst that can happen to you is to have your toes stick out in the cold. But you should lock your door securely, because there may be some maniac around who identifies with Procrustes and skulks in the hallways with a bone saw.

As for the Bed of Ware, it was an enormous bed, famous in England in the sixteenth century and mentioned by Shakespeare in *Twelfth Night*. One of my sources says it was ten feet nine inches in length and breadth. Another says it was twelve by twelve. Anyhow, it was somewhat larger than king size, perhaps emperor size. It was the special feature of an inn in, as you might guess, Ware, and was rented out to three or four couples who insisted on sleeping all in one bed, being either gregarious or afraid of the dark. According to legend, anyone who slept in the Bed of Ware was likely to be pinched and prodded by fairies. If you felt something during the night and heard a burst of high-pitched laughter, that was probably it.

These are only a few of the more interesting things

about beds. You would be surprised how uninteresting some of the less interesting things are. At any rate, the next time you go to bed you might give a little thought to what you are lying on.

AFTERTHOUGHT:

In connection with beds, probably the most touching tribute I have ever written is "My Mattress and I":

> Night after night, for years on end,
> My mattress has been my closest friend.
>
> My mattress and I are cozy and pally;
> There are hills on the sides—I sleep in the valley.
>
> It clearly reveals the shape I'm in:
> Where I'm thin it's thick, where it's thick I'm thin.
>
> Its contours reflect the first and the last of me.
> It's very nearly a plaster cast of me.
>
> I miss my mattress when I am gone;
> It's one thing I've made an impression on.

A sexier title for this poem, I now realize, would have been "My Mistress and I."

Consider the Artichoke

I sometimes wonder whether artichokes were meant to be eaten. The very word disturbs me, especially the "choke" part. I would be somewhat reassured if it were "antichoke," a preventive, instead of what sounds like an artistic method of strangulation. Nor does it help me to trace the word through the Italian *articiocco* and ultimately back to the Arabic *al-khurshuf,* which suggests an enormous, all-encompassing, and perhaps throat-rupturing sneeze.

But what causes me most to question the edibility of the artichoke, or *Cynara scolymus,* is its appearance. What we persist in eating, indeed consider a delicacy, is the flower head of a thistlelike plant. Surely its coarse, leathery texture and sharp-pointed tips were meant by nature to warn us away, or to suggest that if we pluck the flower head at all we should use it in a centerpiece on the table and not serve it on a salad plate.

And yet we boil it in salted water for forty minutes and

serve it up. The very fact that it must be boiled for forty minutes is further proof that it was not meant to be eaten. Encouraged by their success, gourmets may yet try this treatment on pine cones, boiling them until soft and then bearing them triumphantly to the table, where eager guests sit salivating.

Our way of eating artichokes increases my doubt that they were intended for more than decoration. One by one, we tear off what botanists describe as their "large oval involucral bracts" (a far from appetizing description) and scrape away the flesh near the base with our front teeth. Fangs bared, we revert to the primitive, even to the animal.

It can hardly be the taste of the artichoke that attracts us. Whatever taste it has we disguise by plunging each bract into mayonnaise or drawn butter before biting into it. It might be the pleasurable act of eating, the reversion to the primitive mentioned above, a kind of gastronomic atavism. Or it might be the fact that we get such a teasing, titillating little with each toothy scrape. This is comparable to extracting the sweet fluid, drop by drop, from honeysuckle. A cup of the stuff would be nauseating. Similarly, the heart of the artichoke is too easy, and many, after working their way to what might seem their reward, lose interest.

Sometimes, at a fashionable dinner party, I briefly stay my own gnawing and furtively look around at the other guests as they work on their artichokes. In my mind's eye, high-style dresses and tailored suits become tiger skins, crudely fastened by thongs. I shudder. "Would you like to finish this?" I ask, pointing to the artichoke I had barely begun to dismember. Someone, already down to the heart, is almost sure to look at me gratefully and ask, "Are you sure you don't want it?"

But the most astonishing thing about the artichoke is

how it looks when one has finished eating it. In place of the tightly balled flower head is a large dish filled with leaves, each bearing teeth marks so plainly that a dentist could identify the eater if a crime had been committed and he were called to testify in a court of law.

The artichoke is the only vegetable, if vegetable it is, of which there is more after it has been eaten.

AFTERTHOUGHT:

I have never had an unfortunate experience that turned me against artichokes the way an occurrence in my childhood turned me against peas. When I was about ten years old I ate a pea that was abnormal. It had somehow or other wrapped itself around a cocklebur and grown to peahood that way. All the other peas mashed up nicely in my mouth, as peas are supposed to, but this pea-cocklebur, or cocklebur in pea's clothing, stuck firmly to my tongue. It was painful. More than that, it was frightening. I had no idea what it was, a pea never having stuck to my tongue before. It might be a tack, a piece of glass, or a very small crab.

I screamed, and my mother and father dropped their forks (they did not, I am happy to say, eat peas with their knives) and hurried to my rescue. There was no need to ask me to open my mouth. You can't scream with your mouth closed. Besides, I didn't want to take a chance of getting my tongue stuck to the roof of my mouth.

My father tried to reach in and pull the pea-cocklebur off my tongue, but I gagged and he had to give up.

"Get the tweezers!" he commanded my mother, sounding like a surgeon giving orders to a nurse in the operating room.

My mother ran to the bathroom, grabbed up the tweezers, and brought them to my father.

"Open wide," my father said to me, now assuming the

role of a dentist. Then he reached in with the tweezers, caught hold of the object on my tongue, and pulled it off, along with a few taste buds.

"Well, I never," my father said, "a cocklebur inside a pea!"

He thought of taking it to the state agricultural station, or sending it to the Smithsonian, but never got around to it.

As for me, I have never enjoyed peas since. A pea probably wraps itself around a cocklebur only once in a hundred trillion times, but I don't trust the law of averages.

I may not be very fond of artichokes, but at least I have never had an artichoke bract stick to my tongue.

Looking Over the
Overlooked Elbow

For no particular reason, I have lately been thinking
of the female elbow. Perhaps I have been thinking
of the elbow out of perverseness. By this I do not
mean that I am perverted or that I have an elbow fetish
or anything of the sort. It is merely that so few have given
any thought to the elbow that it seems high time to give
this important part of the body its due.

The female breast has been widely photographed and
highly praised. Sometimes, indeed, it has been highly
photographed and widely praised. At any rate, both
height and breadth have entered into it. The female leg,
too, has been pictured and described without stint. (Had
a stint been of any help, I am sure it would have been
used also.) But the elbow remains unsung and largely
ignored.

One reason may be that the female elbow is so much
like the male elbow. It is not so different, for instance, as

the male chest and the female breast, no matter how you look at it. The female elbow may be a little softer and a little smaller. But there is nothing very sexy about it. Freud, who saw something Freudian in just about everything, completely overlooked the elbow. So, also, did Havelock Ellis and Krafft-Ebing. If there is anything dirty about the elbow, it can usually be washed off.

Discouraging as this is, the female elbow is with us to stay. It is part of the whole package. You can't take it or leave it; you have to take it. Perhaps I am especially mindful of the elbow because the German word for elbow is *Ellbogen* or, in its earlier form, *Ellenbogen*. What interests me about this is that I knew a girl in high school whose name was Ellen Bogen. If anyone were to have distinctive elbows, comparable to a forty-two-inch bust, it should have been Ellen. Her elbows ought to have been especially large or firm or well shaped or something. But as I think back on it, or them, I remember them as just ordinary elbows; and if any of the boys turned to look at Ellen, it was not her elbows that caught their eye. I was one who always turned and looked, and I know. Ellen had a peculiar but attractive wiggle as she walked, and by the time I had finished looking at this, she was too far away for me to notice anything special about her elbows.

If anyone who reads this is named Ellen Bogen, she should not feel unduly self-conscious. After all, an elbow in French is *un coude,* and though I have never known anyone named Un Coude, or Ann Coude, the word has an appealing sound. Of course it takes a little of the thrill out of it when you realize the word is masculine. This means, I suppose, that French women have male elbows, which is somewhat unsettling to anyone who had thought of French women as being especially feminine. On the other hand, this shows how dangerous it is to say of some luscious creature, "She is every inch a woman." Remember those elbows, at least when you are in France.

Elbows, in case you have never noticed, are much like knees, except that they work backward. That is, they bend in the opposite direction. If you are despondent about something, just think how much worse a fix you would be in if your knees bent the way your elbows do and your elbows bent the way your knees do. Walking would be difficult, though you would be able to scratch your stomach with your toes, should you wish to. Shaving oneself would be almost impossible, and this would be a boon to the barber business, though a barber would have to stand with his back to the client in the chair and shave him while looking into a mirror.

Elbows and knees have one thing in common. They are both joints. It was Lady Astor, I believe, who once said, "Next to a hamburger stand, a woman's knee is the ugliest joint in the world." But this is the opinion of a woman, or a Lady. Actually, the female knee is something the normal man, and perhaps even the abnormal man, can gaze upon with pleasure. Women know this, and that is why they keep raising and lowering the hemline of their skirts, in a kind of now-you-see-it-now-you-don't game. The female knee is attractive in itself, being smooth, sometimes dimpled, and pleasing not only to the eye but to the touch. The knee is also stimulating, because when you get as far as the knee, you think you are beginning to get somewhere. Whatever Lady Astor may have thought, Lord Astor probably had other ideas. Indeed, it may have been because of Lady Astor that he never said publicly what might have made an even more interesting quotation than his wife's.

But what of the knee's fellow joint, the elbow? The elbow is, after all, higher placed than the knee and perhaps has been unduly demeaned. Though I must confess that my inspection of the female elbow has had little or no effect on my libido, I think a few good words can be said for this portion of the anatomy. In the first place, all elbows are not alike. Some elbows are too fat; some are too bony. A woman with good elbows—neither too fat nor too thin and dimpling nicely when the arms are extended—has a little something extra. But she should not expect them to attract a throng of admirers.

If I have been unfair to the female elbow, it may be that I am conditioned by Western society. After all, the back of a woman's neck is considered really exciting by the Japanese. To touch the back of a woman's neck in Japan is considered to be getting sexually intimate. I know, because once, in Kyoto, I playfully put my hand on the neck of a Japanese woman at a party and she screamed and fell to the floor. She shouted something in Japanese —perhaps, "He tried to rape me!"—and the situation became pretty tense. Fortunately someone had the presence of mind to explain to the woman (and to her husband) that in America the back of a woman's neck is really not all that important.

What I am getting at is that in some cultures the female elbow may be both a sex symbol and an erogenous zone. I do not know how it is in Samoa, for instance, or New Guinea, and I have not had a chance to run through all of the books by anthropologist Margaret Mead and look up "elbow" in the index. It may well be that in certain parts of the world women keep their elbows carefully swathed or veiled. A dress with sleeves that, as a woman moved her arms, afforded a tempting view of the under side of the elbow, would have the same impact as cleavage. Daring fashions might include the sheer sleeve with a peekaboo effect. For women with deficient elbows, there might be falsies. Or for women willing to work at it, hormone creams and exercises might be advertised in such terms as: "Why be flat-elbowed? Guaranteed to increase your elbow measurements by as much as two inches." There would be Before and After pictures.

In such a society a woman with outstanding elbows would obtain high fees as a professional model. She would be a cover girl for the leading magazines, her elbows prominently displayed. Pictured in the centerfolds of magazines, she would exhibit her elbows in dozens of tantalizing poses. Censorship might, of course, force her to hide the tips of her elbows with pasties, but a man with any imagination at all could get a pretty good idea of what was underneath.

Meanwhile, back in America, where the cult of the elbow has made no progress whatsoever, the female elbow is still chiefly used as an instrument of self-defense. Though a woman is advised when attacked to use her knee in a quick thrust to the groin, the elbow can be effective when applied to the rib or the solar plexus. A woman may try to follow up the knee to the groin with the elbow to the groin, but unless she is quite short, this is likely to be a downward blow that will have little if any effect as a deterrent. Nonetheless, the elbow is a supplementary weapon, assuming a woman wishes to defend herself or at least play hard to get.

One reason the female elbow may not have entered the sexual scene is that, unlike a woman's bosom, waist, and hips, there is uncertainty about how and where to measure it. Do you measure the elbow up and down, across, or around? Do you measure it when the arm is extended or retracted? Despite increasing interest in female minutiae, this question of measurement makes it unlikely that the elbow will, in the near future, figure prominently in the promotion of starlets or in Miss America contests.

Nor is it likely that we shall hear a red-blooded male exclaim, "Boy, did you ever see such a pair of elbows?"

At any rate, let us be happy that elbowroom is not a part of the house where old elbows are kept.

AFTERTHOUGHT:

Having written about the elbow and, in another article, about the lips, I am looking for new worlds, or anatomical areas, to conquer. Lately I have been thinking about toes. My thoughts about toes were stimulated by a news item in which a biologist was quoted as saying that, from lack of use, in sixty-five centuries man (and I presume woman) will have no toes. Let me turn to verse, which is something I frequently do when I become emotional, and carry the biologist's speculation further:

> It has been ages, goodness knows,
> Since early man hung from his toes,
> Possessing digits so prehensile
> He curled them round a stone utensil
> Or with them idly scratched his chest,
> Which hair protected like a vest.
> In sixty-five more centuries
> Of toes not used for climbing trees
> Or walking much, feet will grow blunt
> And look the same in back and front.
> Nor is this all. We see a day,
> With automation here to stay,
> When fingers will be merely bumps
> On hands, and hands but skimpy stumps,
> And, evolution's march incessant,
> Legs, arms, and torsos obsolescent.
> Then heads will float (oh, eerie sights!)
> And send out beeps like satellites.

If, however, what is least used goes first, I am inclined to believe it will be our heads. Eventually, and it may not take sixty-five centuries, instead of our being only heads, we may be only toes. I leave you to conjecture about the male toe and the female toe, living in happy toegetherness.

The Author on TV

Every author knows how important it is to have his book promoted on television. He dreams of a lively interchange with Johnny Carson, a probing interview by Dick Cavett, or—a sure boost to the bestseller list—the merest mention, in the old days, by Ed Sullivan. Usually he has to get onto the show, but with Ed Sullivan it was enough to be pointed out in the studio audience, asked, "Won't you stand up, please, so everyone can see you?" and receive Ed's ultimate accolade: "Let's give him a *really* big hand!"

It might be helpful to a new author, about to appear before the television cameras, to know what to expect and how to conduct himself. Let us suppose that, thanks to the timeliness and the controversial nature of his book *How to Build Better Bird Baths,* he has been invited to ' appear on a television program. Without in any way detracting from the importance of his book, it might be remarked that his publishers have paid a tidy sum to a promotion firm to get the author on *some* TV show, *any* show.

When the author arrives at the television studio, he will be directed to the make-up room. There a heroic attempt is made to cover up the bags under his eyes, the hollows in his cheeks, and other evidence of the hard life of an author. For some reason, known only to television make-up artists, the lips are covered with a light coat of a pale substance that makes it difficult to smile and increases the resemblance to a corpse. The author looks better, no doubt of it. But he should not expect too much. This is make-up, not plastic surgery, and his nose will not be straightened or his ears moved closer to his head.

Before meeting the host of the show, the author is instructed in how he is to tiptoe around the cameras and over coils of cable to his chair, when the cue is given. These instructions are given so that he will (1) not make any noise and (2) not break his neck, in that order of importance. He is also told which camera he is to look at: the one with the little red lights. Then he is given a release to sign with no time to read it. Finally he is told the names of the five other guests. This comes as something of a surprise, since it is only a half-hour program and he thought he was being interviewed in depth.

Now he meets the host of the show, and they have a chance to get acquainted during a ten-second chat.

"What do you want me to ask you?" the host asks.

It turns out he hasn't read the author's book. In fact he hasn't seen it. Either the publisher failed to send him a copy or the book was intercepted by the switchboard operator, who needed something to hold down a pile of papers.

But the author, by good fortune, has a copy. In fact he has been clutching it so tightly and perspiring so profusely under the studio lights that the colors have begun to run in the jacket. The author presents his copy to the host, making a mental note to be sure the publisher replaces it. The host thereupon reads the blurbs on the jacket, glances at the title page, and feels pretty well prepared, or as well as he usually is.

On the show, the author is the last of the six guests, and each of those preceding him has run over his allotted time. Thus instead of having a full four minutes, he has two minutes and a half. During that time he:

1. Corrects the host on the pronunciation of his name and the title of his book. ("It's *Better Bird Baths,* not *Bitter Bird Baths.*")

2. Starts to answer the very searching and completely unexpected question, "Why did you write this book?"

3. Stops in mid-sentence when the host puts his hand on his arm and says, "We'll be back as soon as we hear an important message from our sponsor."

4. Starts to answer another challenging question: "Do you keep to a regular writing schedule?"

5. Stops in mid-sentence when the host puts his hand on his arm and says, "I'm very sorry, but we're running out of time and we'll have to bring this fascinating discussion to a close. In the five seconds remaining, could you summarize the main ideas of your book for us?"

6. Starts again, but is aware of a man with earphones, a clipboard, and a stopwatch crouching under the camera directly in front of him. The man is making frantic gestures, drawing his hand across his throat as if threatening suicide, or possibly murder. At the same time the host puts his hand on the author's arm again, but this time squeezes it hard, simultaneously saying, very rapidly, "Thank you for being with us. Good-by everybody. Be sure to watch us again next week."

While someone unfastens and removes the author's neck microphone, one of the other guests comes up.

"That sounds like an interesting book of yours. I'll

have to read it when it comes to the library."

Next up comes the author's wife. She has been in the studio audience, watching the monitor.

"You were great, darling," she says, trying her best to sound sincere. "But I wish you could have got in some of the interesting things you had planned to say about your book, such as the name of the publisher and the price."

"I just didn't have time."

"I suppose not. But why didn't you look at the camera? You were always turned to one side, and you know you look better head on than in profile."

"I looked straight at those little red lights, the way they told me to."

It turns out he had been looking at the cameraman's eyes. They were pretty bloodshot.

So the author goes home and spends all evening with cold cream and facial tissue getting that make-up off his face.

The next day he casually drops into the local bookstore, hoping the proprietor will say she saw him on TV. He starts with some subtle hints, such as, "Did you happen to watch TV yesterday?" Or even, when this fails, "Did you see me on TV?" He is a little crestfallen when the owner of the store says she knew he was on TV but there was a movie on at the same time, one she had seen only once before, and she felt she just *had* to watch it.

"How are the books going?" he asks.

"Fine," she says enthusiastically, thinking he means books in general. Then, when she realizes he means his own book, a gloomy look comes over her face. "It just isn't moving," she says. When she says it isn't moving, she means it isn't selling. You don't move a book, in the language of the trade, by shifting it from one shelf to another.

"I thought maybe my being on TV would help," the

author says wistfully.

"Well, not yet," she says.

"Maybe it's too early to feel the full effect," he says.

"Maybe so," she says, but her heart isn't in it. Anyhow, a bona fide customer has come in and wants attention. Authors, she has learned, don't buy books.

The author stays in the bookstore awhile, but is more and more depressed to see so many people buying every book but his.

"If I had been on the Johnny Carson Show or the Today Show, instead of a local station," he thinks, "things would have been different."

They would have. People would recognize him on the street and maybe even ask, "Aren't you the author fellow I saw on the Johnny Carson Show?"

"Yes," he would say modestly. Here, he thinks, is someone who knows about my book. Perhaps he wants some more details, things I didn't have time to go into on the show.

"Did you have some question in mind?" the author asks.

"Yes," the man says. "What's Johnny Carson really like?"

AFTERTHOUGHT:

Appearing on TV is known as "supporting your book." Every author is mindful of the truism, "Support your book, so that your book will support you." On the ordinary talk show (and there is no such thing as an extraordinary talk show), the author is scheduled last, after the movie stars plugging their new movie, after the comics plugging their nightclub act, after the singers plugging their new album, and after most viewers have turned off their sets and gone to bed.

Several TV celebrities whose shows I have appeared on

are no longer on TV. They are now writing books—which they hope to plug on someone's TV show. It will serve them right if they get on after the movie stars plugging their new movies, after the comics plugging their nightclub act, after the singers plugging their new albums, and after most viewers have turned off their sets and gone to bed.

Yes, I know it is not the host of the talk show who schedules the guests, it is the producer. All right, then let the producer write a book. . . .

Time and Time Again

"Time is money" is an honored, I might say time-honored, saying. Like many another truism, it goes back to Benjamin Franklin, and will be found in his *Advice to a Young Tradesman,* published in 1748.

The relation between time and money is firmly established. We speak of "saving time" and "living on borrowed time." We are as fearful of wasting time as we are of wasting money. "Nothing is so dear and precious as time," wrote Rabelais, who also observed that "lack of money is as bad as a disease." Money burns your pocket, and time lies heavy on your hands. We buy on time. There comes a time to pay. And so on.

Recently I thought I would put the "Time is money" aphorism to a test. Going to our local bank, I filled out a slip at a center table, then walked past the various windows marked "Notes," "Escrows," "Loans," and "Commercial" and stopped at one that seemed to me appropriate.

"Good morning," I said to the pretty young lady at the window. It seems to me that bank tellers are getting prettier and prettier, either because there is so much competition, in this day of tight money, between the banks and the savings and loans, or because, as I get older, I become less exacting. Girls who would have looked attractive to me ten years ago now look gorgeous, and girls who would have looked homely, now look quite attractive. It has got so that I enjoy going to the bank, even when my account is overdrawn.

"Good morning," the girl at the window said cheerily, showing a row of white, perfectly formed teeth. I had already noticed that she seemed perfectly formed in other areas. "May I help you?"

"Yes," I said. "I want to make a deposit."

"Good," she said. "Have you made out a deposit slip?"

"Yes," I said, pushing the slip toward her, under the iron grating, and enjoying watching her bend over to pick it up.

She read the slip carefully, and reread it. Then she looked up, puzzled.

"I can't make this out."

"Can't you read my writing?" I asked. "Maybe I should have printed it."

"Yes, I can read your writing, but I don't understand it," she said. "What do you mean by 'One year, twenty-three weeks, and four days'?"

"Just that," I said. "That's the amount I want to put in."

"But how many dollars?"

"This is the Time Deposits window, isn't it?"

"Yes."

"Then I'm at the right place. I want to deposit some time. I figure I have saved one year, twenty-three weeks, and four days by scrimping and cutting corners and not wasting a minute. I want to deposit it and start earning interest."

"But—" she started to protest before I interrupted her.

"But nothing," I said firmly. "Time is money. One of our Founding Fathers, Benjamin Franklin, said so more than two hundred years ago. Let me deposit this and get out of here. I'm wasting time, and I can't afford it."

To make a short story even shorter, I got nowhere with the girl at the Time Deposits window. She called the chief clerk, and I explained it all over to him. The chief clerk took me to the vice president, and I explained the whole thing again but got nowhere. I shouldn't say I got nowhere. I got into the vice president's office, which I had never been in before. I also got a calendar, a leather-bound address book, and two ballpoint pens.

"I want to deposit some time," I said once again, looking the vice president straight in the eye.

"I'm sorry," the vice president said, "but the only thing deposited here is money."

"Time is money," I said. "And I want to deposit some."

"Time is *like* money," the vice president said patiently. "When you leave your money with us for a certain length of time, it earns money for you." I could see why he was vice president and probably in line for president and then chairman of the board.

"How about that Time Deposits window?" I asked. I can be pretty stubborn when the occasion arises, and the occasion had arisen.

"It doesn't mean what you seem to think it means," he said. "But to avoid confusion in the future, we'll change it."

"To what?" I asked.

"To Deposits on Time, I guess," he said.

"Then all the other tellers will handle tardy deposits?" I asked.

"Yes," he said, willing to agree to anything to get me out of there.

Finally I left, but not before the vice president had given me a gold-plated identification card, a letter opener, a budget book, and two more ballpoint pens.

I felt my time had been well spent.

AFTERTHOUGHT:

What a difference one little word can make, even that commonest of words, the article "the." I have in mind the difference between being asked "Have you time?" and "Have you the time?" The second, of course, is asking for the time of day, and can also be worded, more subtly, "Have you a watch?" Having a watch, however, does not always mean that you have the time, or the correct time, since your watch may be fast, slow, or stopped. What I cannot recall ever being asked is the considerate question: "Have you time to tell me the time?"

If time is money, and I say, "I have all the time in the world," I should be richer than J. Paul Getty and Howard Hughes combined. But, since I am self-employed (a euphemism for unemployed), I haven't even the opportunity to work overtime and be paid time-and-a-half. However there are compensations. I do not have to be on time. Nor do I have to punch a time clock. I can kill time, if I wish, without being made to serve time. Of course all timeservers are not locked up, though perhaps they should be.

But I have given enough space to time, if not enough time to space. I must bring this to a close. And, you will say, it's high time.

They Won't Let Me
Stop Smoking

E ver since the Surgeon General's report on the dire
effects of cigarette smoking, I have redoubled my
efforts to quit. If only I could puff on a cigarette and
not inhale, that would be some improvement. But inhaling
is precisely what I do—though I never lift a cigarette to my
lips.

You see, I go around inhaling other people's smoke. I
don't mean I go around *looking* for it. I simply go around,
and wherever I go someone is smoking. The only way I
can stop inhaling tobacco smoke is to stop breathing—
something that even the Surgeon General doesn't advo-
cate.

I try my best to avoid smokers. If, for instance, I am
on a commuters' train, I sit in the car with a No Smoking
sign. But, alas, the sign lacks the authority of, say, a No
Parking sign. I have never seen a policeman write out a

smoking ticket for a person puffing away unconcernedly under a No Smoking sign.

On airplanes, where there is no such thing as a No Smoking car, I generally find myself wedged between two smokers—in the middle of a row of three seats. If my row is on the right side of the plane, the smoker by the window is a left blower, blowing out of the left side of his mouth, and the one on the aisle is a right blower, blowing out of the right side of his mouth. The only way I can escape is to place my head beneath my knees and breathe the unpolluted air under the seat. More than once a sympathetic smoker has misunderstood my trouble. "Here, take this," he has said, offering me a paper bag from the pocket in back of the seat.

Smokers, I have noticed, smoke especially hard when they are thinking. Instead of doodling on a note pad or a tablecloth when engaged in intense cerebration, they narrow their eyes, purse their lips, and shoot the smoke out in a long, sustained jet that will reach the face of a non-smoker eight or ten feet away. The moment the non-smoker sees the smoker narrow his eyes, he should narrow his also—not to look shrewd and thoughtful but to keep from being temporarily blinded.

I have encountered these smoker-thinkers most often at meetings. I remember a recent round-table discussion at our church. The topic was "Thinking of Others." There was thinking, sure enough (there had to be, since it was right there in the title), and this brought out the matches, cigarettes, pursed lips, and meditative jets of smoke. One of the non-smoking ladies present, who was obviously pregnant, suddenly turned pale and left the room. Since she never came back, she didn't get the helpful list of suggestions drawn up by our secretary, one of the smokers, on how to be considerate of others in our everyday relationships.

If there is any time I enjoy breathing smoke less than any other, it is when I am eating. At lunch counters it is curious how the person next to me is invariably a chain smoker, and how the air conditioning always wafts his exhalations right in my direction. Bobbing and weaving in an effort to get out of the direct line of smoke, I have more than once been pegged as a common drunk. "And at this time of day, too," some fussy patron is likely to observe, nervously lighting another cigarette.

Sometimes my lunch-counter companion tires of his cigarette when there is still an inch of good smoking to go, and rubs it out in the ashtray—but not completely out. There it lies smoldering, throwing off noxious, or at least nauseating, fumes. I dare not reach over and extinguish the thing; it's still his cigarette, and he may decide to take another pull on it. So I let it burn down to the filter, watching it as if it were a fuse. By now the smoker has lit up another, and the fresh smoke mingles with the fumes given off by the dying cigarette. This makes an interesting combination of odors, and I keep my mind off my queasy stomach by trying to separate the two.

I have thought of ways of getting back at smokers, such as carrying an atomizer full of a mixture of garlic, Limburger cheese, and extract of skunk, and countering each cloud of smoke with a spray of my own. However I doubt that it would have any effect against that impenetrable smoke screen.

Whenever I try to dissuade a smoker from smoking, out of apparent interest in his health, and bring up the subject of cancer, I usually get a stony look and "They're *my* lungs."

My reply, if I had the courage to make it, would be, "Yes, but it's *our* air."

AFTERTHOUGHT:

This article, which appeared in the *Reader's Digest,* brought me the most letters anything of mine has ever elicited. Ninety-nine percent of the letters were from non-smokers, smokers apparently being too busy smoking to write. I have space to cite only a few of the more creative or vehement.

A man in Arizona advanced the interesting theory that, at least as regards minor ailments, the smoker builds up an immunity and is less affected by his own smoke than the innocent (and untoughened) bystander. While the smoker goes healthily along, until he is struck down by lung cancer or heart disease, the occasional inhaler of the smoker's smoke is afflicted by such "non-smoker ailments" as "loss of appetite, constipation, eye troubles, back pains, and irritability." The Arizonan himself had all of these afflictions.

A fellow non-smoker in Rhode Island thought we should band together in a new political party. His one stipulation was that I be its candidate for President. It is true that I have important qualifications for that high office: I am native born and over thirty-five.

A woman in Oregon suggested that the warning required on each package of cigarettes be expanded to include: "and may be harmful, or at least disagreeable, to those around you." She also insisted that cigarette smoking is the real cause of smog.

A man in Ohio wrote that his wife is allergic to his smoke, which makes her deathly sick, but he is unable to give up the habit. So when he smokes he stays close to the living-room fireplace and exhales up the chimney. Of all my correspondents, he would seem to be the most considerate—or cowardly.

A Vermonter proposed adoption of some such widely promulgated slogan as "Smokers of the world ignite. You have nothing to lose but your friends." If possible, he would have it set to music. . . .

Once I read, with some satisfaction, that the smoking habit goes back to breast feeding. The smoker, no matter how mature and sophisticated he may think himself, is reverting to infancy. This spurred me to one of my very best inventions for the man who wants to quit smoking. It is a female breast (replica, that is) made of the uncannily skinlike substance of which they make those cuddly dolls. This breast may be hung on the wall, like a picture, at mouth height, and the smoker who has the urge to drag on a cigarette need merely to step over to the wall instead. "Great for the home or office. Sold singly or in pairs." I described this, in some detail, in an article called "The Wall Weaner," which I decided not to include in the present sampling of my work.

Color Me Blue

I'm not dreaming of a white Christmas, I'm dreaming of a green Christmas tree.

The other day it seemed time to buy the annual tree. Stores and streets had been decorated for two months, and the tinsel was beginning to look a little tarnished. Christmas carols had been syruping over the radio and TV since Thanksgiving. Christmas presents had begun to arrive from people who were a little forehanded or a little late, the latter being those who had finally got around to sending *last* year's Christmas present.

So I went to the nearby shopping center, where a corner of the parking lot was being used to sell Christmas trees.

"I want to buy a Christmas tree," I said, going up to the man in charge. As soon as I said it, I realized this was a little absurd. The lot was covered with Christmas trees, and there was obviously nothing else for sale.

"All righty," the man said, and I tried to overlook it. After all, it was the Christmas season, a time of goodwill

179

toward men, and I should be kind to people who say things like "All righty" and "Yes indeedy" and "Hello there" and "Good-by now." But I must confess I was a little on edge, and selecting a Christmas tree takes all of one's poise and judgment. It is a Big Decision, made only once a year, thank goodness.

"How large a one do you want?" the man asked, waving toward his little forest.

"About eight feet, I think," I said. The ceiling of our living room is ten feet, and I could have got a tree nine feet or so; but I had to consider fastening the star on top. Also I have a fear of heights, and if I get up more than two rungs on a ladder, I become dizzy. "Yes, about eight feet," I said again, having visualized the room and the tree and the ladder.

"And what color?" the man asked.

"What colors have you?"

"Blue, white, and pink," he said.

"Haven't you a green one?"

"No," he said. "What do you think this is, a nursery?"

"You mean you are all sold out of green Christmas trees?"

"No, I don't stock them."

"You don't stock green trees?"

"That's what I said."

"But green is the natural color of Christmas trees."

"Not on this lot," he said. "What makes you think green is their natural color, anyhow?"

"I've never seen a white fir or spruce growing in the woods," I said.

"Don't be silly. White trees are trees with snow on them. Haven't you ever seen a tree all covered with snow at Christmas time?"

"Not in Southern California," I said, "except maybe up in the mountains."

"But everybody here in Southern California comes from the East or the Middle West. And that's the way they remember trees at Christmas time. I'm from Michigan, myself, and that's the way I remember them. All white."

"But haven't you noticed they are green out here, with no snow?"

"Can't say I've seen a tree up close since we left Michigan. Look around you. See any trees?"

I looked around the shopping center, with the freeway running alongside, and had to admit I couldn't see any, except the Christmas trees on the lot.

"You've got me there," I said. Then I thought a minute. "But how about those pink trees? Do you have pink trees in Michigan?" I was just a wee bit sarcastic.

"Mister," he said, "trees are pink lots of times. Take when the sun is just coming up. Or when the sun is just going down, at sunset."

"I've seen trees at sunset," I said, "many times. And I've seen them a few times at sunrise, though I'll admit not so often. They might be a little yellow or golden, but they're not pink."

"Look again," he said. "That's what lots of people tell me. But I tell them to look again, take a good close look. They think because the sun is yellow, the trees are yellow. But that's not so. They're pink. It's because of the haze or something. Anyhow, you don't think I could sell yellow Christmas trees, do you?"

"No," I said. "I suppose not. But you could sell green Christmas trees. You could sell me one right now, if you had it."

"Let's not go back over all that again," he said, a little testily. "As I told you, I haven't any green Christmas trees. There's no call for them. I can't put in a whole slew of green Christmas trees, expecting oddballs like you to turn up. I could be left with a whole batch of them on my

hands, and lose my shirt. Did you ever try to sell a Christmas tree on December twenty-sixth?"

"No," I said. "I suppose it would be difficult."

"Difficult?" he said. "It's impossible."

"All right," I said, "it's impossible. But you can't expect to sell every tree. You have to allow for a few left-
overs."

"No," he said. "I don't have a single leftover. I start
marking them down after 6:oo P.M. on the twenty-fourth.
I've sold a tree for as little as twenty-five cents, around
midnight. I'd rather get two bits than nothing."

"It's a risky business, I guess," I said sympathetically.
"And I know you can't afford to take any chances."

"That's right," he said. "And I'm not in this thing for
fun. It's not my regular business, you know. I don't sell
Christmas trees the year around. But I like to pick up a
few extra bucks. I've got five kids, and they've all got to
have Christmas presents." Then he added, "So how about
buying a Christmas tree? It's about time to close up."

"I'd like to buy a tree," I said. "But I don't want a
white one or a pink one, despite all you've told me about
the snow and sunrises and sunsets. As for those blue trees
over there, they make me sick. Does anyone ever buy a
blue Christmas tree?"

"Lots of people. It's one of my best sellers. I suppose
you think a tree never looks blue."

"Of course it doesn't. Unless maybe it's feeling sorry
for itself, out on a lot like this with Christmas so close and
nobody taking it home to a nice warm living room."

"Very funny, mister. Not let me tell you, trees are blue,
and I mean really blue, lots of times. Like when it's just
starting to get dark."

"And I suppose when it's really dark, trees are black.
Why don't you sell black Christmas trees?"

"Mister, do you want a Christmas tree or don't you?
I'm closing up in about two minutes."

I had to have a Christmas tree, and this was my only chance to shop for one. Besides, I felt sorry for the man, with five children and a lot of unsold Christmas trees.

"I'll take that pink one over there," I said, pointing to a tree that was a nice shape and about the right height. "How much is it?"

"Six fifty."

"All right. I'll open the back of my car and you can help me put it in."

So, for the first time in my life, I bought a pink Christmas tree. But before I left the shopping center I made one other purchase. A spray can of green paint. We are having a green Christmas after all.

AFTERTHOUGHT:

After that episode, I did something else I swore I would never do. The next Christmas I bought an artificial Christmas tree. It came in parts, and it took all my mechanical skill to follow the instructions and stick the right branches into the right holes in the imitation trunk. The first time, I got a little mixed up and put the short branches in the low holes and the long branches in the upper holes, and the tree looked like a huge green fly-swatter. But finally I got the thing right, and everybody thought it looked even more real than a real tree. The plastic needles even dropped onto the floor and had to be swept up.

In the words of Joyce Kilmer, "Only God can make a tree." But only man can make the kind you take apart and put into a box and save for next year.

Reading Habits of
the Young

Once there was a high school teacher who got her students to read *Silas Marner* and enjoy it. She went about it in an unusual way. She told her students that it was a naughty book; that it was written by a woman named Mary Ann Evans who preferred to be called George; and that they might get carried away by the story and miss the author's message. Her clincher was that it was available only in a cheap paperback.

The students read *Silas Marner* with such gusto that this teacher is thinking of trying the same technique with *Moby Dick* and *Ivanhoe*.

The lesson to be derived from the above is that young people will read almost anything if it is not required, and if it is practically guaranteed not to do them any good. The best recommendation for a book, to a teenager, is not from the reviews of literary critics but by word of mouth, so long as the mouth is not that of a parent, teacher, or librarian.

When it comes to magazines, teenagers will read almost any of them, but they especially like the magazines to which they do not subscribe. These they read at the magazine stands (so called because that is where one stands while reading magazines for free), completely oblivious of the hostile looks of the proprietor. Sometimes, while reading magazines, they do not stand but sit. Usually they sit on the stack of magazines from which women shoppers are not strong enough to push them in order to get a copy.

The younger set cannot understand why adults insist on reading under a strong light. All that glare must be why so many older people have to wear glasses. It is much easier on the eyes to read lying on the floor instead of sitting stiffly in a chair and putting all that strain on the spine.

Another thing about adults that is pretty silly is the way they read without the radio on and without simultaneously watching TV. The really versatile teenager not only reads, listens to the radio, and watches TV all at once, but at the same time carries on a telephone conversation, munches a candy bar, and drinks from a bottle of pop. He hasn't forever, and he needs to make every minute count.

"Some books are to be chewed and digested," wrote Francis Bacon. If the teenager could only eat each page, after reading it, he would be really happy, lying there on the floor in the dusk.

AFTERTHOUGHT:

It would appear from this that I do not think highly of the reading habits of teenagers. But the contrary is true, because teenagers are the most faithful readers of my books, thereby displaying intelligence and good taste.

They even *buy* my books, being able to shake down one or the other of their parents for the price, and anyone who buys a book of mine is a friend of mine. True, I wrote a book, *Through Darkest Adolescence,* in which I examined adolescence clinically, as a disease. "You wouldn't hit a sick person, would you?" I asked. In their more rational moments, teenagers know I am right. Or, as one teenager wrote me, "You've got my number." I'm glad they don't have *my* number, or they would be calling me up any hour of the day or night.

High school students sometimes choose me as the subjects of a paper they have to write in a history or literature class. They choose me as the subject of a paper in history because I have written a number of irreverent spoofs of history, and not, I hope, because they consider me an historical personage like Charlemagne or Oliver Cromwell. One high school student wrote me: "I thought for a while that all American authors are either dead or dull. Then I found you. Thanks for not being in either category." (He spelled it "catagory.") "Since you are neither dead nor dull, it's hard to find articles or books about you. Please send me a list of such works, so I can pad my bibliography. Then maybe my teacher will pad my grade." This young man had "pad" on his mind, but his heart was in the right place. I sent him some materials, and he later wrote me that he got an A on his paper. It must have been the subject.

A Short Note
on Long Hair

I N this, the Age of Hair, I have seen no mention of what
seems to me to be a matter of genuine significance. It
affects, among other things, the question of male or
female superiority. Certainly it is more important than
many things I have read about recently in newspapers
and magazines or heard about on the talk shows on television.

The question that has been nagging me and that I felt
I must find the answer to if I am to regain my peace of
mind, is simply this: Can a woman grow hair longer than
a man can grow his beard? I suspected that a woman could
outdo a man in this department, but could not be sure.

Most records can be established in a fairly short time,
perhaps in minutes and certainly in not more than weeks
or months. Consider the record for the number of persons
who can crowd into a telephone booth, the number of

oysters that can be eaten at one sitting, or the length of time contestants can teeter and totter on a teeter-totter. Growing hair, however, is something that takes years. It would be silly to tell a group of male and female competitors, "Ready, set, go. Now see who can grow the longest hair."

We must therefore search the annals of history, and this I have done. After considerable research, including asking my friends, I have discovered that the longest feminine tresses were those grown by a certain Miss Owens in the nineteenth century. They measured eight feet three inches. I have been unable to learn anything more about Miss Owens, such as her first name, her other measurements, or what she did—other than cultivate her hair. I would especially like to know whether she ever married and, if not, whether her hair somehow stood, or got, in her way.

On the other hand or, in this case, chin, the longest recorded beard was that of Hans Langseth, a Norwegian immigrant to North Dakota. At the time of his death, in 1927, his beard had reached a length of seventeen feet six inches. That makes it more than twice as long as Miss Owens's hair. I am sorry if this comes as bad news to Women's Libbers and female chauvinists. But facts are facts.

This is admittedly a sketchy report. Many questions remain. For instance, to what did Mr. Langseth and Miss Owens attribute their hirsute success? Could it have been heredity? Diet? Massage? The competitive spirit? And while Miss Owens may have been able to pile her more than eight feet of hair atop her head in a spectacular hairdo, what about Hans Langseth and his seventeen-and-a-half feet of beard? Did he wrap it around and around himself boa fashion? Or did he fold it neatly and stow it in a large pouch suspended from his neck?

Another thing, Hans Langseth's beard was donated to the Smithsonian Institution. But where is Miss Owens's hair? Did she refuse to part with it?

Anyhow the central question is now answered, and my mind is somewhat at ease. A man, we learn, can grow a beard longer than a woman can grow hair. Or perhaps I should say "has grown" rather than "can grow," for this is only the record of the past. Taking up the challenge, some woman may even now be on her way to surpassing Miss Owens and indeed growing hair longer than Mr. Langseth's beard. If there is such a woman, however, there is probably also a man somewhere who will carry on where Hans Langseth left off.

But what if we change the ground rules a little and, instead of comparing the length of a man's beard to that of a woman's hair, make it simply hair to hair? It just happens that the hair of Swami Pandarasannadhi, the head of a monastery in India, reached twenty-six feet in 1949. For all I know, it's still growing. On the other hand, the longest beard on a woman, who turns out to be Janice Deveree, born in Kentucky in 1842, petered out at a mere fourteen inches. Hair or beard, women come in a poor second.

Delilah's motive may not, after all, have been a desire to weaken Samson. It may have been jealousy.

AFTERTHOUGHT:

As for me, I shall never set any records for growing hair. I tried a mustache once, but found my upper lip too short. The space between my nose and my mouth gets overcrowded very easily, and if my mustache had been allowed to grow to normal proportions it would have made breathing through my nose difficult if not impossible.

I also tried a beard once, but the hair came in red and

I was laughed out of court. What was I in court for, I don't recall, but it was an embarrassing experience.

Where I have the hardest time growing hair is on the top of my head. Though in my youth I had a thick head of hair, as well as a thick head, in my late thirties I developed what is known as a receding hairline. That is, I began to have more and more forehead and less and less scalp, scalp being defined as "that part of the human head *usually covered with hair*." I distinctly remember, though I have tried to forget, the first time someone referred to me as bald. It is a little like being called middle-aged when you think of yourself as young, or being called fat when you think of yourself as husky. It does something to your psyche, and if your psyche is like mine it may never recover.

A barber once told me that baldness is caused by poor circulation in the scalp and poor circulation is caused by having a head, like mine, that bulges out on the sides. This stretches the scalp tight. The blood vessels have a hard time of it. The ideal head for loose scalp and good circulation, and therefore good growth of hair, is a head that is narrow—best of all, one that gets narrower as it goes up.

If I had a head that came to a point, no doubt I would have excellent circulation in my scalp and plenty of hair. But would it be worth it if I were called "Pinhead"? Or if, when I put on a hat, I poked a hole through it?

I read an article once, in fact I read it twice, asserting that baldness is an indication of virility. I wanted to believe it, but would have felt better if the article had been accompanied by a photograph of the author and a few biographical notes. Unfortunately, my mental picture of the fellow is a weak little man, completely bald, dominated by a big, lusty wife.

But I have to go now, to get the groceries and do some other errands. "Yes, dear, I'm on my way."

Now if I were that swami, with hair twenty-six feet long. . . .

'N'

A word that fascinates me is 'n' or, in quotation marks, where it should probably be kept when not in active use, " 'n'." One reason it fascinates me is that it is not in my dictionary, or at any rate I have been unable to find it. It is not under " ' " nor is it under "n," though in looking for it I found that "n" can be several interesting things that had not occurred to me. For instance, "n" can mean "not" when used in such a word as the obsolete "nam" ("ne am" or "I am not"). And "n" is the past participle ending of strong verbs such as "blown" and "known." Then of course there is the mathematical use of "n" as an indefinite number, as in "to the nth degree."

But unless my dictionary is incomplete—and it is a large unabridged one that seldom fails me—" 'n' " is not listed.

Yet I know there is such a word. I have seen it, over and over, in the expression "wash 'n' wear." Sometimes, it is true, it has appeared as " 'n" in "wash 'n wear," but it has looked wrong to me, as if something were lacking. Indeed, I have written to several advertisers who have used " 'n" instead of " 'n' " and told them I thought they had misspelled the word. But since I have been unable to find the word in my dictionary, I have had no proof, and it is perhaps just as well that I received no reply to my letters.

The word " 'n' " seems to be used more and more widely. At first I noticed it only in "wash 'n' wear," but now I find it in "fish 'n' chips," "sugar 'n' spice," "tall 'n' handsome," "soft 'n' furry," "rise 'n' shine," and many another combination. I have come to be quite fond of " 'n'," constantly seeking it out and hailing it, when I find it, as an old friend.

But in one way the word is beginning to get on my nerves, and on the nerves of others. I find myself trying to pronounce it—not in combination with other words but all by itself. The best I can do is to place the tip of my tongue against my gums in back of my upper front teeth, open my mouth slightly, and grunt. Friends who hear me as I walk around unconsciously doing this (I am conscious as I walk around, but unconscious of what I am doing) say I sound like a hog with a stomach-ache. Probably they mean a hog that will wind up as the ham on a plate of ham 'n' eggs.

AFTERTHOUGHT:

I have referred to the miswriting of " 'n' " as " 'n," with the second " ' " left out. I should add that sometimes " 'n' " appears as "n'," with the first " ' " omitted. In the first instance " 'n' " lacks a tail, while in the second " 'n' " lacks a head. Once in a great while I come upon " 'n' " written simply, "n," by someone obviously quite unfamiliar with the word and confusing it with the letter "n." Such a person, leaving off both the head and tail of " 'n'," will be unable to make head or tail of my discussion of the word, 'n' probably has given up before this.

Houses I Have Known
and Loved

My wife likes a one-story house, without a stairway to climb or to clean. I like a two-story house, where my bedroom is not at street level and I have a feeling of privacy. My wife likes a light, bright house, with much glass to let in the sunshine and to permit her to see what is going on outside. I like a dark house, with small windows and wood paneling and a sense of snugness. My wife likes a new house, with all the modern conveniences. I like an old house, with character and a lived-in flavor.

We have compromised. We have the kind of house my wife likes: one-story, bright, and new. After eighteen years in an old two-story colonial that I loved—creaking stairs, sagging backsteps, leaky roof, and all—we have built a very modern house with a cement-slab floor and great expanses of glass. I must confess I enjoy showing guests around and pointing out such up-to-date features as the electrically operated garage door (when the electricity goes off, we are stuck) and the one-way glass in our bedroom. This latter permits us to look out but prevents anyone from looking in. I would as soon forget the first week, when the glass was installed the wrong way around.

As I say, I enjoy taking guests on a tour, but when I refer to this structure of glass and cement as my home, the word comes hard. Home, to me, is still that two-story colonial that some usurper now lives in and that I occasionally drive by, with wistful looks. After a dozen or so years in this present house, I may be able to think of it as home, but I doubt it. However, my wife is happy, and I am happy she is happy, and I guess that's all that really matters.

But what I am leading up to, quite aside from personal preferences, is that a family has considerable impact on a house and a house has considerable impact on a family. People build houses and, to some extent, houses build people.

Going back to my own childhood, I am aware that each house I lived in had a certain influence on me. There was, above all, my grandparents' big old house, with its huge porch that went around two sides, its front and back stairways, and its third-floor hideaway to which my grandfather, a gentle little man with a lame leg and a droopy mustache, retreated when my grandmother was too much for him. My grandparents' house had a pantry, the focal point of which, to me, was the jar filled with peppermints, within reach if I stood on a chair; a dining room where aunts and uncles I rarely saw at any other time gathered at Thanksgiving and Christmas; and a music room that one entered by parting a curtain of beads which always gave me the feeling of going into a Chinese opium den. It was a big house, though I have no doubt that to a little boy it probably seemed bigger than it really was. It was a house of mystery and adventure, full of rooms and hallways to explore.

No other house in my life did so much to stimulate my imagination. But other houses made their contribution. For instance, there was the house where I lay sick for many weeks, and came to know my bedroom as a prisoner must come to know his cell. Every stain in the ceiling, every crack in the plaster walls, remains etched in my memory. And then there was the house with the sun porch and the potted plants that my father complained got more attention from my mother than he did. My father liked to nap on the couch in the sun porch, and when he napped he snored, and when he snored I got up close and watched, fascinated by the noises and the flutter of my father's cheeks. My father had business worries, and the only time I saw him truly happy and relaxed was when he was there in the sun porch, snoring amid the ferns and the rubber plants.

There were many other houses in my childhood, my father being a restless man and my uncle an architect who had few clients outside the family. And there have been several houses since I grew up and married and had children. But only one house—that two-story colonial we lived in for eighteen years—has seemed like home.

Each house I have lived in has done something to me and changed me a little from what I would have been had I not lived in it. Not only ease and happiness but discomforts and unpleasantnesses made their mark on me. For instance, I remember the time my mother and father and I lived for six months in one room above our newly built garage. We were building a new house, and had no place else to live until it was finished. This took longer than we anticipated, because the contractor left town— taking my father's down payment with him. Those six months in the same room with my parents brought us together, all right, but I was glad when the house was finally completed and I had my own room.

This leads me to an observation about privacy and community living in a home. Ideally, there should be both. Sometimes it is necessary for two children to share a room, and I think this can be good for a while. But the time comes when a child wants a room of his own. And though I remember how we frowned at some of the pictures on the walls of our son's room, and deplored the general messiness of our daughter's, I am convinced that a child's room should be his castle. There should be the minimum of intrusion by the parents, except perhaps to keep the place from becoming a fire hazard. Certainly there should be no imposition of taste regarding what is on the wall or undue concern about what is on the floor instead of on a hanger in the closet.

The hands-off policy is difficult, and can hardly be applied one hundred percent. But it helps a parent to know that time will ultimately set things aright. Patience and good example will do more good than nagging.

I have said that a child should, if possible, have his own room and be let alone in it. Sometimes this matter of one's own room applies not only to children but to parents. Once I wrote a bit of verse called "Sequence":

> The nocturnal life
> Of a man and his wife
> This pattern quite often assumes:
> First two in a bed,
> Then each in a bed,
> Then sleeping in separate rooms.

After a lecture in which I recited these lines, a little old lady came up to the platform.

"You left out the last step of that sequence," she said.

"What comes after sleeping in separate rooms?" I asked, taken aback.

"Sleeping in separate rooms with the doors closed," she said.

Well, I have never got to that last stage. As a matter of fact, my wife and I got as far as sleeping in separate rooms and then reverted to sleeping in the same room. The reason we slept in separate rooms for a while was not that we were angry at each other or tired of each other. It was because I like to read in bed but she doesn't. When I read in bed, my light bothers her, despite spotlights, blinders, and all the other devices we have experimented with, and she is unable to go to sleep. But now, having made a choice between books and my wife, I have given up reading in bed, and we share a bedroom again. She seems to like it better that way. And I was getting lonesome, too. I may not be as well read, but I am better wifed.

The ideal home, as I have suggested, has many possibilities for both privacy and coming together. It seems to me unfortunate when children immediately after dinner retreat to their rooms, while mother and father settle down in the living room. The most popular room in many homes is what is called the family room or the den. More relaxed and better adapted to living than the often misnamed living room, it is a place where members of the family see one another under friendly, informal circumstances before retiring to their own rooms.

The trouble is that it is hard to imagine a family room, these days, without a TV set. I have nothing against TV. I am an ardent viewer myself, concentrating on panel shows, spy thrillers, comedy, and sports. But it would please me if there could be a brief blackout of TV each evening. If I were more knowledgeable about electronics I would fix, or unfix, our set to accomplish this. During this period all of us could talk together about whatever was on our minds.

Let me make one other point about the relationship of people to the house they live in. My mother was a compulsive housekeeper. There was a place for everything, and everything was in its place. Her floors were so clean that, as guests used to say, "You could eat off them," and I was always waiting for her to test their sincerity. My mother looked forward to spring not because of the birds and flowers but because of the excuse for spring cleaning. Her year-around cleaning was thorough by any standards, but spring cleaning was something to marvel at. Rugs were hung on the clothesline for beating and airing. Pictures were taken off the walls. Almost everything but the piano was moved outdoors or to another room. The floors were either waxed or painted, and for a few days we tiptoed in and out over newspapers.

I suppose it is in reaction to this kind of housekeeping that I have always liked houses that are casual, even a little cluttered and helter-skelter. I think it is possible for a house to be too neat, neat to the point of being stiff and impersonal. Not that I suggest going very far in the direction of slovenliness. I have in mind a sort of selective disorder. Not dirty socks in the center of the floor, but books left wherever they were being read, and perhaps a sweater over the back of a chair.

Alexander Pope, writing in the so-called Age of Reason, liked nature "methodized," with carefully planned walks and clipped hedges. The more romantic Wordsworth liked nature natural—paths following the slopes and valleys of the terrain, perhaps the trail made by cows or sheep, and trees growing wherever they took root.

I am somewhat romantic about houses. I like them easy and relaxed, as natural as man-made things can be. And I want the combination of privacy and joining together that is possible when a house fits the family that lives in it.

A man is known by the company he keeps. He is also known and affected by the house he lives in. Our son, who grew up in that old two-story colonial, where he had a back bedroom with two small windows opening onto a garden, does an interesting thing when he comes home to our new house of cement and glass.

The moment he walks in, he starts closing the draperies to cut the light and to keep anyone from looking in. Then, having gone to his bedroom, unpacked his clothes, and strewn them over the bed and chairs and floors, he feels at home.

I understand.

AFTERTHOUGHT:

Among the houses I mentioned was one that had stains in the ceiling that I gazed upon when, as a child, I lay sick in bed. I should add that the stains looked like animals, an overhead zoo that helped me pass many an hour. Out of my memories came a nostalgic article, "Heavens Above," that was published in the *Saturday Review*. This in turn led to a book for children, *Animals on the Ceiling*. What made the book seem worthwhile was a letter, forwarded by her second-grade teacher, from a little Mexican-American girl who said she had three brothers and four sisters. "We have lots of animals on our ceiling," she wrote. "But the rich kids don't have any."

Who Says I'm Hard of Hearing?

My wife and children have the absurd idea that I'm hard of hearing. The truth of the matter is that they mumble. They don't enunciate clearly. This has come about only in the past few years, and seems to be getting worse. I doubt that anything has gone wrong with their speech mechanism. More likely it's just laziness or carelessness.

"I wish you would speak more distinctly," I say to my wife.

"You need a hearing aid," she says.

"What?" I ask. I thought she said, "You need a key ring made."

"You ought to have your ears examined," my wife says.

"That isn't what you said the first time," I say, showing how alert I am. Or perhaps, "I don't know anyone named Yottav Ursamin. Sounds like a Russian or a Turk."

"I give up," my wife says.

"What was that?" I ask. But she turns aside and resumes her conversation with our daughter, the two of them using some form of gibberish I am unable to understand.

Feeling left out, I go back to watching television. It's an old movie, starring Fred Astaire and Ginger Rogers, and I notice how distinctly everyone spoke in those days. Even the words of songs come through clearly.

"Turn that thing down!" my wife yells from the next room. "It hurts my ears."

"Did you say something?" I ask.

"Never mind," she says.

"I think so too," I say. I thought she said, "Clever mime," referring to Fred Astaire, and I am willing to go along with her, to avoid an argument. Actually, it has always been Fred's dancing, and not his mimicry, that has appealed to me.

The practice of slovenly speech is not limited to my wife and our children. Many of my friends and business associates are beginning to speak in this same muted, mushy way. Take the assistant manager of our local bank. I had some business dealings with him the other day.

"Do you want a receipt for this?" he asked.

I thought he said, "Do you want to sleep on this?" Probably he wanted to give me a little time to think things over before I made a decision on an important money matter, involving as much as ten dollars.

"No," I said. And then a little later, when he gave no signs of having finished his business with me, I asked, "Aren't you going to give me a receipt?"

"But I thought you said you didn't want a receipt," he said.

He is a tricky fellow, and you have to watch him. I wouldn't be surprised to read in the paper some morning that he had embezzled a large sum from the bank and fled to Argentina.

Besides this increase in poor enunciation, I have noticed that the bells they put on telephones aren't as good as they used to be. Only a few years ago I could be outside, washing the car, and hear the phone ringing in the house, with all the doors closed. Now I can be only a couple of rooms away, and the ring is so feeble that I don't hear it at all.

"Can you get the phone?" my wife asks. She is in the shower, with the water running, but she hears it. It must be that water is a good conductor of sound.

"What?" I ask.

"Oh, I'll get it," she says. By the time she has turned off the shower and wrapped a towel around herself and run to the phone, it has stopped ringing. If it ever *was* ringing. Often I think she imagines it, except that sometimes when she gets to the phone she starts talking at once, without dialing.

It *must* be something wrong with the way they make bells these days, and not just the ones for telephones. Or maybe the electric power isn't as strong as it used to be. Anyhow, our front-door bell is so faint that I can't hear it, even when I am only a few feet away. I have thought of having it fixed, but it saves me a lot of trouble with door-to-door salesmen.

Of course there was the time I was alone in the house and the postman came with a registered letter that I had been eagerly awaiting. The next morning I found a note that the postman had pushed under the front door. "Rang repeatedly," read the note, "but nobody home." Then there was a check mark alongside "Held at Post Office." Maybe I will have to get that doorbell fixed. . . .

As I said, my wife and children think I am getting hard of hearing, but I know I hear as well as ever. I could hear a pin drop, if it weren't that they make pins so much lighter these days.

AFTERTHOUGHT:

Things have been getting worse lately. People are speaking so low and mumbling so much that I have taken to getting up very close to them and cupping my hand around my ear. I know it looks absurd, for a person who is not hard of hearing, but it may shame them into speaking up and enunciating better.

Like so many things today, the fault is in the family. My father used to tell me, "Speak loudly and distinctly. You'll never get anywhere in life if people can't hear you." He became more and more insistent about this as he grew older. I probably owe my resonant, carefully phrased speech to my father's constant correction. Parents don't take the time now to get their children to speak so that they will be heard and understood.

I may overdo it a little, because sometimes during a conversation people back away from me a couple of feet They even say, "You don't have to shout."

At least I *think* that's what they say.

The Depopulation
Explosion

Man is at least a million years old and beginning to look it. He has lost most of the hair that once covered his body and kept him warm without his having to decide on the color and the fabric and whether to have two buttons or three. Back in the old days, he had only one button and it was permanently set in the center and unaffected by styles. Nor was there any question about whether to have side vents or a center vent. Year after year, he went along with the same old center vent, and it worked very well.

The change has been so gradual—just a little every few thousand years—that man is hardly aware of how much he has deteriorated. Once his teeth were so strong that he could gnaw a bone as well as any of the other animals. If his incisors and canines stuck out a little, enabling him to take a bite without having to raise his upper lip, so much the better. To have had orthodontia would have struck him as ridiculous. Never in his wildest dreams did he imagine what it would be like to have a tooth drilled or to try to keep an upper plate from slipping during a spirited conversation.

In early times, man walked everywhere he went, and not on the advice of his physician. Not until the domestication of the horse did he get where he wanted to go sitting down. Not until the invention of the wheel were there any unfortunate consequences from exceeding the speed limit or turning without signaling. Walking or running from place to place, breathing air uncontaminated by sulphur compounds and hydrocarbons, he kept himself in shape without steam baths, massage, or a morning routine of exercises.

His good health was also furthered by a sensible diet, consisting of never having quite enough to eat. Not cooking his food, he did not lose the essential juices, nor did he become upset if he ordered a three-minute egg and got a two-minute egg. There was no such thing as well done, medium, and rare—only extremely rare, or raw. It did not occur to him to worry about salt, sugar, or cholesterol. Vitamins did not have to be added, because they had not been taken out. His only concern about food was getting it.

Man at first wore no shoes. He went barefoot everywhere, and not because he belonged to some protest group. Since he wore no shoes, he had no corns, ingrown toenails, athlete's foot, or need for a podiatrist. Thanks to calluses that grew thicker instead of thinner, he never required resoling. If his heels were run over, they were his own heels and no one dared say they looked slovenly and should be fixed.

Man was, in short, in fine physical condition. He slept without sleeping pills and kept regular without taking anything that could be spelled backward. If he caught a cold, he simply waited until he got over it, instead of disturbing his sleep to take an antibiotic every four hours. He breathed deeply, from force of habit; and, despite a highly developed sense of smell, was never offended by bad breath or perspiration odors. Nor did he worry about offending. After all, there was no perfume or after-shave lotion to help one sex recognize the other, and the olfactory sense was on its own.

Since early man lived close to his work, he was spared the wear and tear of commuting. Self-employed, he was never upset by having someone less competent promoted over him. Nor was his blood pressure made to rise dangerously at thoughts of the income tax, Big Government, and giveaway programs.

When the decline began is not known precisely. It was slow at first. It was hundreds of thousands of years before man became overweight, lost his muscle tone, and started going to a psychiatrist. What is clear is that, once the decline began, it became increasingly rapid. Man has deteriorated more in the past fifty years, perhaps in the past five, than during any previous millennium.

This decline, both physical and spiritual, has shown such increased rapidity with each generation that it can hardly be an accident. There is too much evidence of a carefully thought-out plan.

Obviously, man has decided to do away with the human race. Not all at once and openly, but gradually and by subtle, ingenious means. He could get it over quickly with a thermonuclear holocaust, but that would be too evident, too easy, and rather heavy-handed. Intelligent creatures on some other planet might be watching. They would expect something better of the race that has produced fifty-two flavors of ice cream, drive-in banks, and the electric toothbrush.

Why man decided to exterminate the human race is not really known. A hint of the reason, however, may be found by anyone who watches TV commercials and, for purposes of research, stares at himself in the bathroom mirror immediately upon arising.

At any rate, it is now clear what is going on. Man is engaged in an intricate, many-faceted plan to rid the earth of what was once called Homo sapiens but now, in an increasingly sexless society, is referred to simply as Homo. Under cover for many years, perhaps because it was not yet perfected, the plan is now out in the open. There is no longer any reason to stand aloof or to leave it to the specialists. Extermination is for everyone.

There are many ways you may make your contribution to this worthwhile project. The easiest, employed by many persons, is simply to sit. Before invention of the chair, people sat on stones and logs and the ground. Everything they sat on was either hard or rough or damp, and we can understand why they were always getting up and walking around. Besides, they had to go get whatever they wanted, there being no home delivery or room service.

The straight chair made it easier to sit for long periods. But it was the upholstered chair, followed by the molded-plastic chair, that made it possible to sit for hours on end. A contribution was also made by the rocking chair, a contrivance that gave ambitious people the feeling they were on the move and getting somewhere without getting up. Of recent years the chair has become a home within a home, its equipment including a built-in vibrator and an ice-making machine. Some of the later models have bathroom facilities. Once settled, the sitter has no reason to leave. If the chair is placed in front of a television set, with a remote-control device for changing channels, so much the better, because now there is something to do, other than to think, while sitting.

Thanks to year after year of sitting, you become comfortably soft and flabby, with a stomach that you cannot keep from patting and rubbing. "It's mine," you mumble happily, "all mine."

More important, the cholesterol count rises in the blood, the arteries harden, and you can look forward to a coronary or an embolism that will bring you to a swift end. When this comes, you will not even have to get up from your chair, if it is the latest type, the kind that folds up around you and can be moved directly to the slumber room.

Paradoxical though it may at first appear, exercise can be as effective as sitting. As a matter of fact, the two may be profitably combined. First, sit for several years, until the walls of the arteries have thickened and the heart has grown unaccustomed to strain. Then suddenly take up a vigorous exercise, such as broad jumping or weight lifting. While you may get nothing more than a hernia out of all this, there is always the possibility of something a little more spectacular, such as a ruptured aorta.

Even if you take up exercise gradually, by choosing the right exercise you can do wonders. Consider bicycle riding. Riding a bicycle in heavy traffic or after dark without a light will, in a gratifying number of cases, result in a fatal accident. Riding a motorcycle is even better, since a motorcycle has room for a passenger, and the average accident will thus dispense with two persons instead of one.

Among other sports highly recommended are sky diving, sports-car racing, and karate. A small private plane or a glider affords endless opportunities for exciting crashes, especially if you play a game of chicken, heading straight for a cliff at full speed, to see whether it will turn to one side before you do.

One of the nicest combinations of sitting and exercising

is isometric tension performed in a wheelchair, where you
are confined with casts on both legs after a skiing accident.
How is this done? You wheel your chair up until you can
reach out and press against the living-room wall. (Be sure
to set the brakes.) Day after day, you press with all your
might, building up the biceps, triceps, and pectoral
muscles. If you are faithful to this exercise, pushing at
the wall during every waking hour, you will not only
develop magnificent muscles but, one memorable day,
bring the ceiling tumbling down on your head. This is
approximately what Samson did, setting a good example
for future generations of physical-fitness buffs.

The automobile, of course, offers interesting possibilities to be of service to the cause. Until consumer advo-
cates got to poking into things that were none of their
business, and vote-conscious legislators pushed through
restrictive bills, automobiles were admirably constructed.
They had spearlike steering columns to pierce the chest,
unpadded dashboards to crush the vital organs, and
splintering glass to take care of the eyes.

But all is not lost. If safety belts are not fastened, a
front-seat passenger can be catapulted through the windshield. If doors are not locked, they can spring open and
dump passengers into the path of an oncoming car. One
belt that will be found helpful is a belt, or several belts,
of Scotch or bourbon just before crawling into the
driver's seat. The two cars you try to drive between will
really be only one car, and this can lead to interesting
consequences.

Only a short time ago man believed that air, which at
that time was invisible and odorless, was present in unlimited quantity. Unless there were clouds, as far as he
could see he could see nothing, and he assumed all this
was air. Pollution of air that stretched out to infinity was
a discouraging prospect—some said impossible.

Fortunately, man was wrong. Scientists have discovered

that there is only a thin envelope of air around the earth.
The amount of air is definitely limited. Complete contamination is fairly easy.

What joy there was when this discovery was announced!
Those who had been rather halfheartedly sending pollu-
tants into the air, convinced that it was a hopeless, never-
ending task, went back to work with new zest. They held
their heads a little higher, there was a little more spring
in their step. It was not their imagination. Their eyes *did*
smart a little more and it *was* a little harder to take a deep
breath. There was a fullness in their hearts, almost match-
ing that in their lungs. Some burst into song, delightedly
discovering how soon this brought on a fit of coughing.

As a means of destroying the human race, air pollution
is extremely attractive. It has the three prime requisites:
subtlety, gradualness, and total effectiveness. Slowly, but
not too slowly, it ruins the lungs. There is no noise, no
mess, as there would be in a nuclear explosion. There is
no chance, as there would be in the employment of bac-
teriological resources, that some persons might escape by
building up immunity.

It is the universality of this method that gives it its
greatest appeal. After all, everyone must breathe. There
is no way to avoid the intake of polluted air, except by
stopping breathing. Of course if everyone could be
counted on to stop breathing for as little as half an hour,
the job could be done quickly and efficiently. There
would be no need to bother with the laborious and expensive process of air pollution.

But there would be a few spoilsports who would refuse
to cooperate. There would be others who, despite their
good intentions, would after years of breathing find themselves hooked. Still others might try to kick the habit, but
would backslide after experiencing the discomforts of
withdrawal.

What, you ask, can I do to help?

Write to your state and federal representatives and members of the Supreme Court, pointing out that legislation forcing you to install an antismog device on your car is an infringement of your personal liberties. If you are hauled into court for failure to install such a device, take the Fifth Amendment. Refuse to say whether or not you have such a device. And do not let anyone find out by looking at your car. The Fourth Amendment, on unreasonable searches and seizures, protects you from this.

Keep careful account of the voting record of your congressman. If he leans toward federal legislation to require installation of exhaust devices and otherwise shows himself an opponent of air pollution, do your best to see that he is not re-elected. He is probably a Communist or a dupe of the Communists. The Communists, as you know, want to keep the human race going, to have something they can make trouble for.

Now, finally, a quick look at water pollution.

Until recent years, efforts at water pollution seemed to be making little or no progress. With water covering seven-tenths of the earth, the magnitude of the project discouraged all but the most dedicated and stouthearted.

Little by little, however, the work has gone forward. Results are beginning to show. As one leading water polluter said during a television interview, "It has been a long, hard struggle, but I think we have turned the corner. Given continued support by an aroused citizenry, I am confident we shall win."

Industry, of course, spearheads the drive, sending a vast tonnage of waste matter into rivers, lakes, and other waterways. But the humblest individual plays a part, adding his mite to the sewage that gathers volume as it goes from house to house and at last, a raging torrent, empties into the sea near some populous bathing resort.

As the housewife finishes her laundry and empties her

washing machine of the last load of foamy, insoluble detergent, she can rejoice in doing more than getting the family's clothing clean. She is helping pollute the water of the nearby lake, thus preventing the loss of no telling how many man-hours previously wasted on the idle pursuit of fishing.

Do your bit with garbage and trash. Your own efforts, added to the good work of huge pipes funneling sewage into the ocean and barges dumping radioactive wastes offshore will, ere long, achieve what we are all after. Someday, even the larger bodies of water will be filled with such quantities of waste that they will be almost solid.

Then man can walk on water, which hasn't been done for two thousand years.

To sum up, with regard to elimination of the human race: We have done well, but we can do better. We are in sight of our goal. One last great push. . . .

AFTERTHOUGHT:

I planned to write a book in the manner of Swift's *A Modest Proposal* and call it *How to Eliminate the Human Race*. After writing about half of it, I became so depressed that I put the project aside and turned to other things. One of these days I may bring this playfully gruesome project to a conclusion, if I am not myself brought to a conclusion first. But rather than make my readers wait, I published this excerpt in *Playboy*.

One of those who wrote to the magazine said, "I nominate Richard Armour for pessimist of the month." I appreciated the honor. Not everyone gets nominated for something for which there is so much competition. Having been nominated, and I presume elected, I would then be eligible to compete as one of the twelve finalists for Pessimist of the Year. The judges would be some of the leading philosophers and statesmen of our time. Who knows? I might carry off the title, the trophy, and the cash.

But alas, the only thing I am pessimistic about is getting very far as a pessimist. I can occasionally write something that passes for pessimism, even cynicism, but it is an attempt at irony—saying one thing and meaning the opposite. The only time I managed this for book length was in *It All Started with Stones and Clubs,* a satirical history of war and weaponry. But Jonathan Swift, who didn't make a practice of trying for laughs, would have thought me, even in this, too good-humored.

Inasmuch as the names Swift and Armour have long been linked, albeit in meat packing rather than literature, let me say something about Swift. He is one of my favorites, along with Chaucer and Mark Twain. Many think that Swift hated the human race, and they cite especially the fourth book of *Gulliver's Travels,* about the Houyhnhnms, in which horses are elevated morally and intellectually above men. He says some bitter things, I grant. But I prefer to think that Swift, like most satirists, loved the human race but was disappointed in it and wanted to make it better. The person who hates the human race drops out and becomes a hermit. He does not stay around, as Swift did, calling attention to its faults and indirectly suggesting improvements.

That, in a minor way, is what I intend to do as long as I can. When my time is up, here is my epitaph:

> I pray the Lord my soul to keep,
> And let me laugh myself to sleep.

About the Author

Richard Armour is one of the most widely read writers of humor and satire in our time. His books, of which this is the forty-fourth, include a number of best sellers and have been translated into many languages. He has also contributed to more than 200 magazines in the United States and England, from the *Saturday Review* to *Playboy* and from *The New Yorker* to the *Reader's Digest*.

A Harvard Ph.D. and longtime professor of English at many colleges and universities, he has lectured or been guest-in-residence on over 200 campuses. As an American Specialist for the State Department, he has also lectured at leading universities throughout Europe and Asia.

In addition to an amazing variety of subjects, he writes in both verse (as in *Light Armour, Nights with Armour,* etc.) and prose, and for children as well as adults. One of his most unusual books is the recent *On Your Marks: A Package of Punctuation,* with a foreword by Ogden Nash, which has been made into an animated film. He is especially popular with students for such books as *It All Started with Columbus, Twisted Tales from Shakespeare, The Classics Reclassified, American Lit Relit,* and *English Lit Relit,* and with teachers for *Going Around in Academic Circles* and *A Diabolical Dictionary of Education.*

Richard Armour is married (as you would discover in *My Life with Women* and *Through Darkest Adolescence*) and lives in Claremont, California.

818	Armour, Richard
ARM	Out of my mind

DATE			
SE 25 '73			
MR 10 '75			
MY 1 '75			
NO 19 '76			
6/78-mrs B			
SE 21 '79			
FE 7 '80			
FE 2 '80		A	